The Wheatley Manuscript

FROM BRITISH MUSEUM ADD. MS. 39574

Early English Text Society.

Original Series, No. 155.

1921 (for 1917).

þis is my child ——— In whom me liketh moost
boþe meke and mylde
Blissed be þ baptist for thi preching
þow pfet apertely þe poyntes of pees
to herode and herodias his deye deuyng?
resones and right þow rekynde on ryfe
þ sayd ful scharply in þi saiyng
And stode stedefastly þ thoght not to fese
he led hym not laufully in his liuyng
for philip his brothir wyf þ he to hym chese
þe wyf þ he chese? gretly gan hym greue .
sittyng on deyse
she made hir doghter tue? and herod gaf hym leue
þi hrued for to haue
Blissed be þow baptist þi name is fulworthy
It betokenith good sire as clerkes us deye
And of many moo matis men may it dispiy
Also so wil lustly listen and beye .
baptist for baptim so saith þe story
Of þ worthy wight þ hath no pere
prophet and aungel he may be callyd holy
And lantern of light þ styneth ful clere

THE WHEATLEY MANUSCRIPT.
BRIT. MUS. ADD. MSS. 39574, folio 15a.

The Wheatley Manuscript

A COLLECTION OF MIDDLE ENGLISH VERSE
AND PROSE CONTAINED IN A MS.
NOW IN THE BRITISH MUSEUM
ADD. MSS. 39574

EDITED WITH INTRODUCTION AND NOTES

BY

MABEL DAY, M.A.

LECTURER IN ENGLISH, KING'S COLLEGE, LONDON
ASSISTANT DIRECTOR, EARLY ENGLISH TEXT SOCIETY

LONDON:

PUBLISHED FOR THE EARLY ENGLISH TEXT SOCIETY

BY HUMPHREY MILFORD, OXFORD UNIVERSITY PRESS

AMEN CORNER, E.C. 4.

1921.

KRAUS REPRINT CO.
New York

OXFORD
UNIVERSITY PRESS

Great Clarendon Street, Oxford OX2 6DP
United Kingdom

Oxford University Press is a department of the University of Oxford.
It furthers the University's objective of excellence in research, scholarship,
and education by publishing worldwide. Oxford is a registered trade mark of
Oxford University Press in the UK and in certain other countries

First Edition published in 1921

Published in the United States of America by Oxford University Press
198 Madison Avenue, New York, NY 10016, United States of America

British Library Cataloguing in Publication Data
Data available

Library of Congress Cataloging in Publication Data
Data available

Original Series, 155

ISBN 978-0-85-991895-4

PREFATORY NOTE

By the courtesy of Messrs. Maggs, I became acquainted with and examined this fifteenth-century MS. in the year 1917. I recognised its value as a collection containing some hitherto unknown poems, more especially the Hymn to St. John the Baptist, which by the kindness of Messrs. Maggs I was permitted to transcribe. It seemed desirable that the volume should be secured for the British Museum. About this time the Early English Text Society lost the valued services of Dr. H. B. Wheatley, who had so well helped forward the Society's work as Honorary Secretary from 1864 to 1872, and as Treasurer from 1872 to the time of his death. It occurred to me that the association of his name with an Early English manuscript would have appealed to him as the best tribute to his memory. By a generous consideration on the part of Messrs. Maggs, and with the help of the Trustees of the British Museum, and the Shakespeare Association (of which Dr. Wheatley was Chairman), supplemented by contributions from a number of friends, we were enabled to purchase the MS. for the British Museum, on the understanding that it should be named " The Wheatley MS.," and that its publication should be reserved for the Society. The text, edited by Miss Mabel Day, is appropriately assigned to the year of Dr. Wheatley's death, and is dedicated to his revered memory.

I. G.

October 28th, 1920.

CONTENTS

PREFACE

Description of the Manuscript.—The manuscript (British Museum,
Add. 39574) belongs to the beginning of the fifteenth century. It is
written on vellum, and contains 88 leaves, which now measure nearly
16 cm. by 10 cm., but which have been much cut down, as can be
seen by the larger initials. The number of lines to a page is generally
19, sometimes one or two more. At the end of every 8th folio, with
the exception of the 24th, a catch-word is written. The length of the
larger initials is two lines of the MS., except in the case of the first,
which extends through eight lines, and that on p. 76, which is four
lines long. They are illuminated in blue, ornamented in red; smaller
initials, such as those of each Latin verse of the *Seven Penitential
Psalms*, and of the verses of *God's Complaint*, and paragraph marks,
are alternately blue and red, the former beginning each page; titles,
where they exist, and the rubrics of *Adam and Eve*, are in red. In
the second part of the MS. all rhyming lines are bracketed in red.
Two poems, VI and VII, are written as continuous prose, the lines
being divided by stops or bars, and the verses by paragraph marks.
In IV the Latin verses are written in a larger and plain book-hand.

The manuscript is written by two scribes, the change taking place
after F. 32 *b*. Both write a book-hand of cursive type, with elements
from charter-hand. The first, whom we may call A, uses a more
ornamental style; the second, B, writes a plainer hand. In particu-
lar, A elaborates the upper loops of letters in the first line of his
page; B, to a much less extent, prolongs the tails in his last line.

Of the ordinary abbreviations, both use $þ^t$, $þ^u$, w^t, for *þat*, *þou*,
with, and employ the ordinary signs for *er* (*re* after *p*; also, by B, in
" where," 76/3, "here," 76/4), *ra*, *ur*, *ro* after *p*. A stroke through
the stem of *p* denotes a following *er* or *ar*, but B also uses a dot on
each side of the stem: per̃esche, IV, 753, per̃seyue, IV, 842, par̃ties,
77/9, per̃auenture, 79/6, 80/17, temper̃al, 90/20, par̃adys, 92/29, as
against the bar in per̃soonys, IV, 952, per̃auenture, 80/33, depar̃te,
85/17. The abbreviated form Iħesu is written by A with a stroke

vii

through the *h*, by B with a mark over the *u* ; in IX, 11, the form is ihē. Neither scribe distinguishes between capital *I* and *J* ; small *j* is used by B alone, in the combination *i j* = *ī*.

The writing of A, being the more ornamental hand, gives more trouble in the interpretation of its abbreviations. Every final *ll* is crossed, and every final *k*, with only one or two exceptions, has a small tick or loop following it; these I have disregarded. Final *g* is sometimes quite plain, sometimes followed by a mark resembling an *es* abbreviation, and so used in " God*des*," III, 128, sometimes it has the loop of this without the vertical, sometimes the vertical without the loop. It may be compared with the mark after " craue," III, 124 (see the Facsimile), and I have considered it as merely ornamental. There is also a final crossed *h*, used only occasionally, as in "swich*e*," I, 150, negh*e*, IV, 146, some nine times in all. This I have taken to represent a final -*e*, as it differs from the others in its infrequency, and in the assistance which, in the two cases quoted, it gives to the metre. It may also be noted that it is used as an abbreviation in " Ih*e*su."

The abbreviation for a nasal presents some difficulty. Undoubted cases are very rare, and generally occur when the scribe was afraid he would not have room for his line, *e. g.* i*n*, III, 20, þa*n*ne, i*n*, III, 63, hy*m*, III, 84, IV, 319. These are almost the only examples, the others, occurring in such words as " incarnacion," " passion," must, I think, be treated as the similar marks, generally extending over two or three letters, over such words as "vpon," " doun," " lantern," III, 134 (see the Facsimile), and considered merely as flourishes.

In addition, we find crossed *l* for *lett*-, II, 275, *s* superscript for *is*, II, 284, the ordinary abbreviation for *us*, III, 6, and a small *e* superscript appended to *r* in " her*e*," III, 48.

B represents the nasal abbreviation by a straight line over the preceding letter, and makes much more frequent use of it. He also uses a small *i* superscript for *ri*, and, in "qu*i*ke," VIII, 15, for *ui*.

The numbering of the stanzas does not appear in the MS. Otherwise, all additions to the text are enclosed in square brackets ; where words or letters are substituted, or their order is changed, the MS. reading is given at the foot of the page. Omissions are marked with a dagger. The lists of different MSS. of the various poems are derived from Professor Carleton Brown's *Register of Middle English Religious and Didactic Verse*. The abbreviations used in referring to the MSS. are explained in the Introduction to each poem ; in every case the expression "all MSS.," denotes all those I have seen, *i. e.* those at Oxford and London.

The contents of the volume are entirely religious. The strictly devotional part ends on p. 75 with the Pater Noster, Ave Maria and Credo, the final prayer on p. 100 being added to fill up the sheet. The choice of the first and last pieces may perhaps be due to the growing devotion to the Holy Name. This was especially marked in England during the fifteenth century, and by 1457 the Feast of the Holy Name is found in the *Sarum Gradual*, though it was only formally sanctioned by Pope Alexander VI, 1493–1503 (Frere, *Graduale Sarisburiense*, 1894).

I. **An Orison on the Passion.**—This poem has not been printed before. It is also found in MS. Bodley 850, Ff. 90–92*b*, written between 1383 and the end of the fourteenth century, which omits ll. 12, 57–62, 147, MS. e Mus. 232, Ff. 62–65*b*, Bodley Add. E. 4, Cambridge Pepys MS. 2125, F. 76*b*, Lambeth MS. 559, F. 134–134*b* (as far as l. 12, ending, "And ȝet thou callid hym thi frend, God send vs charite wi*th*outen ende. Amen."), the Gurney MS., and two Longleat MSS. MS. Add. E. 4 has the following rubricated heading : " In seying of þis orisone stinteþ & abideþ at eue*ry* crose & þinke whate ȝe have seide. For a more deuout prayer fonde Y neue*r* of þe passione, who so wolde abidingly sey it." The crosses are at the beginning of each stanza from ll. 21–57, and at 75, 79, 87, 91, 95, 103, 123, 131, 135, 139, 149. A similar arrangement is found in MS. e Mus. 232, where the poem is also divided into stanzas of 4, 8, 12, or more lines.

The *Orison* has also been identified by Miss Charlotte D'Evelyn as being inserted, with the exception of a few lines which include the opening stanza, in various parts of *Meditations on the Life and Passion of Christ*, now being edited by her for the Early English Text Society, see pp. xxiv–xxvii. I am indebted to Miss D'Evelyn for an early sight of the proof-sheets of her introduction.

The dialect is East Midland ; OE. *ā* rhymes with OE. *o* lengthened, *e. g.* stoon, þeroon, 5, 6, sore, bifore, 21–2 ; once with OE. *ō*, also, doo, 63–4. The infinitive has lost *-n* : be, 17, quake, 35, wepe, 42, goo, 58, knowe, 75. The pp. has generally lost *-n* : doo, 64, bete, 66, bounde, 82 ; on the other hand, we have bygone, 48.

Final syllabic *-e* is preserved ; masculine and feminine endings do not rhyme, with the exception of : knowe, owe, 75–6 ; blys, is, 99, 100, compared with blys, ryches, 113–4. Some lines show hiatus, *e. g.* 30, 31, 65. As the lines are not strictly octosyllabic, it is impossible to say whether every final -*e* was pronounced.

The lines fall into four-line stanzas, which are not distinguished in the MS. The fourth and fifth stanzas have no pause between them; after stanza 14 six lines have been added (see Note); in the case of the first couplet of stanza 26 a variant seems to have intruded into the text. Stanza 35, however, appears to have consisted originally of six lines.

The hymn is more notable for devotional feeling than for poetic art. In general style and dialectal characteristics it resembles "The Symbols of the Passion" (Morris, *Legends of the Holy Rood*, p. 170, E.E.T.S. 46), the latter part of which precedes it in the fragmentary Bodl. MS. Add. E. 4.

II. **A Prayer to the Blessed Virgin.**—This hymn, of which no other MS. is known, was originally in the Northern dialect. OE. *ā*, *a* rhyme; *e. g.* bare, mare, 35–6, brade, made, 73–4, vptane, nane, 89–90. The present participle ends in -*ande* : pray[ande], 155, weldant, 102, both rhyming with "hand." The infinitive has lost -*n*, except "goon," 72, but "goo," 172. The past participle ends in -*n*; vptane, 89, (?) sene, 2. Ind. pr. 2s. ends in -*s* : has, 166. The three pres. pls. in -*th*, hath, 9, saith, 15, 19, which are not in rhyme, may well be due to wholesale scribal alteration of the 3*s*. Northern -*s* into the E. Midland -*th*. It will be noted that they are not in connection with a subject-pronoun.

The metre is too irregular to yield conclusions as to the value of final -*e*, but masculine and feminine endings appear to rhyme pretty freely, *e. g.* vmset, lett, 9–10 ; fayn, payne, 177–8.

The poem marks the highest flight of the medieval devotion paid to the Blessed Virgin, as may be seen from the argument in 37–48. It is also most interesting by reason of its quaintly "conceited" pleadings, as the appeal to the Mosaic Law, 157–66, or the poet's description of himself as "God's love-child," 314 ; and in this respect it distinctly stands apart from the general tone of Middle English devotional literature, and has affinity with the religious poets of the school of Donne.

III. **Hymn to St. John the Baptist.**—Of this interesting poem no other manuscript is known. It bears a close resemblance to the poem entitled "Of Sayne Iohn þe Euaungelist" in the Thornton MS., printed in *Religious Pieces in Prose and Verse*, E.E.T.S., p. 97. Each has eight long alliterative lines, rhyming alternately, a phrase from the end of the last line being caught up to begin the "bob" which follows, but whereas the Thornton poem varies it slightly, our poem repeats it literally, making the eighth and ninth lines rhyme. Hence, where the Thornton rhyme scheme is ababababccdccd, ours is ababababbbcddc. Again, in the Thornton poem the long lines alliterate in pairs, the only exceptions being ll. 199–200, and ll. 45–6, where four lines have been telescoped into two. Our poet makes an evident attempt to do this, especially at the beginning of each verse, but in half the verses there is no sign of it. He is also much more partial to lines alliterating aabb, e.g. II, 1, 8, of which there are 11 or 12 cases; the Thornton poem, nearly double the length, has but three. The "bob," here and in the Evangelist poem, differs from all the other arrangements of short lines in the rhyming alliterative poems by rhyming in pairs instead of triplets, thus following the ordinary Romance 6-line stanza of *Sir Thopas*. The metre is, however, distinctively alliterative, and the lines have but two stresses.

Similarities of vocabulary and phrase can be found in any two alliterative poems. Those here are, however, sufficiently striking to be cited in detail :

Jon Baptist.	Sayne Iohn þe Euangelist.
1–2. borne & forth broght Of a byrde baran.	7. That in Bedleme was borne of a bryde bryghte.
20. Ne no man markyd on molde	2. And of þe molde merkede
26–7. He bring vs to þat blys þer myrthes non mys	8–9, 12. brynge vs to blysse þare beste es to byde ; To byde in his blysse . . . Whare myrthe may noghte mysse.
	106–7. þou broghte thaym to blysse Thorowe mendynge of mysse.
29–30. whan þou were borne bare Of þat buxum body.	156. Then blyssede þe body, bare þare it laye.
62. þat Goddes Sone wolde be bourn of þat body bolde	184. þat ilke body þat hym bare.
73. Faythefull in frestyng	
	73. Bathe frenchipe and faythe to frayste it bese fun.
	237–8. to frayste in þaire fare Faythefull and frendely.
114. þe poyntes of pees.	84. þe poyntis of his preuaté.
115. his dere derlyng.	153. thi derlynge so dere.
136. Goddes darlyng so dere.	
126–7. þi name is full worthy, It betokenith Goddes grace.	138 Thi name es Goddes grace.

Several of these passages, where the same words are used with

a different sense, suggest a vague verbal reminiscence of one poem
on the part of the writer of the other. From the method of alliteration it seems probable that the Evangelist poem was the first. It is
certainly superior in its handling of the story, which in our poem
is exceedingly confused. Possibly the verses are in the wrong order;
5 would follow better after 1, and 3 and 4 might be inverted.

The dialect in both is Northern, OE. $\bar{a}$ rhyming with $\ddot{a}$, but not
with $\ddot{o}$. In our poem there is more use of final syllabic -e: doute, 5;
myrthe, 8, 9; blode, 18, ground, 19; swete, 46; dere, 115. The
only certain example in the Evangelist poem seems to be " mare," 20.

IV. **The Seven Penitential Psalms.**—Of this poem there are
several MSS.: at Oxford, Digby 18 (D), Rawlinson A 389 (R), Ashmole 61 (A), Laud Misc. 174 (L), Digby 102 (D$_2$), Douce 232 (Do.);
at the British Museum, Harley 3810, pt. I (H) (two pages are missing,
containing stanzas 50–55, and stanza 92.7 to the Latin of 99); Royal
17. C. xvii (Ro), Add. 11306 (Ad) (this MS. is complete, except for
stanza 15), Add. 36523 (Ad$_2$), and the MS. here transcribed, Add.
39574 (W); at Trinity College, Dublin, MS. 156 (D. 4.8.) ending at
Ps. xxxix. 13 (so Carleton Brown; (?) xxxviii. 13); also the Longleat
MS., in the possession of the Marquess of Bath, the Porkington MS.
20, belonging to Lord Harlech, Quaritch MS. Item 584, Sale Catalogue 328, ending imperfectly, and in America, J. Pierpont Morgan
Lib. MS. 95 (K). This was edited by Ellis and published by
William Morris in the Kelmscott Press under the title *Psalmi
Penitentiales*, 1894. D, with full collations from R and A, is
edited by Adler and Kaluza in *Englische Studien*, Vol. X, p. 215–55
(*Studien zu Richard Rolle de Hampole*, III). These three, as can
easily be seen, diverge very greatly from our text. Ps. li. (*Vulgate* l.)
also exists in five MSS.: Oxford Douce 141, Vernon (V), edited by
Horstmann, E.E.T.S. 98, Cambridge Dd.1.1, British Museum Add.
10036 (Ad$_3$), edited by Furnivall, E.E.T.S. 15, Edinburgh, Advocates
MS. 19.3.1.

The differences between these versions are very great, especially
in Ps. li. and the following psalms. This was explained by Kaluza
and Adler (p. 225) as being due, in the case of Ps. li. and cxxx.,
to contamination from an older version.[1] This, however, cannot
account for the large variations that exist. For example, of stanza 53

---

[1] In Ps. cxxx (vv. 98–105) the very distinct breaks regularly found after the
fourth line would make it extremely easy for A to omit the last four lines of
each stanza; while a comparison of stanza 53 in A and W shows the different
rhyme scheme of the former to have arisen from a corruption of the latter.

there are at least four different versions, (1) W, K, Ad, D_2, Do,
followed by A with different rhymes in the even lines, but the
same sense; (2) R, Ro, V, Ad_3; (3) D, L; (4) Ad_2; v. 104 has three
versions, (1) W, K, Ad, D_2 Do, H, (2) D, R, Ro, L, (3) Ad_2.
Differences such as these are probably due to individual devotional taste, others are due to scribal errors and misinterpretations.
l. 278, "I stomble as thei that blynde be" becomes in Ad "as de
(= the) blynde be," and in Ad_2 "as doth þe blynde be." Again,
l. 839 reads in Ad, "And we schulle up to heuene hulle," H "hylle,"
Ro "helle," where the meaning is clearly "hill," and the rhyme is
Kentish. In R the line becomes "And we schul up to heuene &
hel," D "telle." With editorial daring, the scribe of the original
of W and K emends to "And gode men schulen in heuene dwelle,"
while A_2, less metrically, has "And crist with is peple to heuen shall
go snell." Many of the variations seem to be caused by imperfect
memory, the rhyming words being retained, e.g. stanzas 12, 13, 19.

Emendations have only been made (1) in cases of evident scribal
error, e.g. the substitution of "but" for "thow" in 15, or the
omission of "hath" in 19, (2) when the omission of a final -e or
-n, or a change in the order of words, or the omission of a word
not grammatically necessary, disturbs the metre, as " stynke[n]," 43,
"sweet[te]," 77, "[vs wasches]" for "wasches vs," 148, "[al]," 253.

Of the various versions, K approaches far more nearly to our text
than any of the others I have seen, though neither is derived from
the other. It is in a Southern dialect, with, as a rule, pr. pl. ind. in
-eth, and several pps. in y-. The only considerable variants it gives,
apart from small scribal errors and variations, are : 572 as scrachenis
(for "Ryȝt as a þing"), 600 Yblessed be that ylke deth, 616 The
turmenturus upon me tere, 687 For he was nothur starke ne stef
(the rhymes are : seeth, beeth, pr. pl. fleeth, stef), 693 How he was
for us, 748 as clerkis calle (for "grete and smalle"), 774 Forsake
us noght wan have nede, 782 My gostly fo wan y schal fle. K
alone agrees with W in 11–16, 75–6, and in the order of 221–4,
where all other MSS. read correctly 223, 224, 221, 222.

In the other large divergences of W and K from D, i.e. 103–4,
231–2, 418–24, 452–6, 477–80, 492–6, 515–8, 719–20, 765–8,
787–92, 826–32, 919–20, Ad always agrees; D_2, Do always agree,
except in 452–6, where they follow R; H agrees, except in Ps. li.,
where it agrees with D; Ro always agrees with D, as do Ad_3 and
V, which comprise Ps. li. alone. Ad is in the Kentish dialect, and

the earliest of the MSS. I have seen ; it is ascribed in the British Museum catalogue to the fifteenth or latter part of the fourteenth century ; D₂, Do are Southern, D₂ belonging to the beginning of the fifteenth century ; H is E. Midland, Ro of a more northern type. L is almost identical with D, and has the prologue stanza.

It is not easy, and often impossible, to decide which of these variants represents the poet's original. It is seen, however, that the MSS. in a Southern dialect, *i.e.* K, D₂, Do, Ad, agree with our text. Of the passages mentioned above, where this group gives different readings from those of D, etc., our group nearly always gives the better reading, though in 765–8, the second line is unmeaning compared with D, " Thoruȝ feiþ and hope & charite," and the last is weak ; while in 452–6 Do and D₂ agree with D, and are unquestionably the better reading, cp. Adler and Kaluza's text :

> Lord, I hertili þee biseke ;
> The þeeues trespasse, it was forȝeue,
> Hangynge on tre his bones breke ;
> A sorrowful herte & a clene schreue (D₂ & clene yshryue)
> Saueþ soule & body eke.

In 231–2 D is more striking, and may be original, in 719–20 there is little to choose between the two passages, but in the others the Southern text seems to me always preferable. I append the texts of these passages as printed by Adler and Kaluza.

> 103–4. Aȝen himsilf his wepyn he wetteþ,
> That casteþ his herte to suche perile (*cp.* Note on this passage)
>
> 418–24. & wickedly wrouȝte aȝeyn þi glory
> Wiþ wordes and wiþ tricchery,
> þou demest riȝt & hast victory ;
> þerfore þi blis now biseche I,
> For tolde hit is in mony a story,
> þat who so trusteþ to þi mercy,
> Haþ endeles blis in memory.
>
> 477–80. A blisful brid was brouȝt in cage,
> Couþe & kid in euery coost,
> Whanne we ben drawen in tendre age,
> To driue adoun þe fendis bost.   (The meaning of this seems altogether obscure.)
>
> 492–6. And þenke on Cristis heued & herte !
> Boþe breste, bodi & bak was bleche,
> How it was bete wiþ scourgys smerte ;
> To rewe on him I wolde reche,
> Alas ! þer may no ter out sterte.   (This is an echo of v. 59.)
>
> 515–8. But certeynli noon such offryng

As of himsilf plesaunt may be.
Thi silf was offrid child ful ʒonge
And aftir don on rode tre.   (Here ours gives the better sense
                                    and is nearer to the Latin.)

787–92. D omits 787–8 and adds at the end
         That it may be to þi likyng,
         The lyf, þat I schal leden here.   (The weakness of the lines
                                                   suggests that they were
                                                   a stop-gap.)
826, 828– And raumsum eke in grete plente . . .
32.   That owʒte be take in greet deynte.
           His blood he schedde wilfulli,
           To make oure former fadir free,
           And alle oure raunsomes bi & by
           He quitte himsilf and non but he.
919–20. Late neuere þe fend oure soulis schende, (see Note.)
         But helpe us alle boþe now and efte !

On the whole it seems therefore that the Southern texts are nearer to
the original poem.

Metre.—The 8-line stanzas of the poem are regularly divided by
a distinct pause at the end of the fourth line. Where this does not
exist, as in stanza 4 in W and in stanza 36 in all versions except
Ad₂ and Ro, one may fairly assume scribal corruption. The lines
consist of four stressed syllables, alternating with one, or frequently
two, unstressed. Final -e has syllabic value in:

(1) weak nouns, hert[e], 128, 194, 262, 344, 349, 405, 465, 514,
herte, 578, 683, 783, 918 (at 569 the handwriting changes), erthe 270,
chirche 651, name 665 (K), tunge 757, wille 923, food[e] 381, bonde
895.

(2) strong fem. nouns : soule 11, 290 (K), 304, 372, 946, rode
195, 406, 518, sight[e] 200, synne 235, 346, 443, 912, speche 307,
strengh[e] 397, myrth[e] 476, hele 481, nyʒt[e] 598, lawe 621, care
706, strengþe 822, 922, blis[se] 936.

(3) Romance nouns : grace 208, 251, 343, 949, gyl[e] (MS. gylt)
310, vice 368, face 424, 897.

(4) strong m. and n. dat. sg. : godde (K) 293, rib[be] 622, þriste
576.

(5) drede 13.

(6) adjs. with vowel stems : oure 460, pore 413, wyld[e] 223.

(7) weak adjs. : fair[e] 694, gode (voc. sg.) 390, longe 244, owne
580

(8) st. pl. adjs. : alle 908, blynde 278.

(9) adverbs : depe 22, dere 15, 184, 536, more 336, oute 72, sore

494, 695. (It is significant, however, that all these except "sore" 494, and the comp. "more" precede a pp., which probably had an original prefix ge-.)

(10) inf. : dampne 158, haue 75, make 20, 109, mende 40, mouthe 143, negh*e* 146, [w]epe 152, etc.

(11) pr. ind. 1 sg. : wexe 212 ; pl. fede 301, passe 775.

(12) pr. subj. : lyke 408, graunte (K) 679.

(13) imp. sg. : byholde 433, clense 402, graunt[e] 471, turne 897, vouche 791, 950.

(14) wk. pt. : hadde 873, schulde 655, 725, seyde 308, sweet[te] 77, tauȝte 716, þraste 582, went[e] 316, wolde 368.

(15) strong pt. 2s. : were 421.

There are only a few cases where difficulty arises : "lyfë," acc. sg. 391, where probably the line is a later variation, and the original is to be found in D "That I may lyue *in* loue & drede" ; "flesch," acc. sg. 428, where the MSS. give many different readings, D, R, A, L inserting "ful" before "freel"; good 361, where we should have to suppose hiatus at the caesura ; theef 589 (see Note) ; God 465, and Lord 794, which seem to be intentional.

Dialect.—The dialect of the poem is East Midland (cp. Adler and Kaluza). There is one Southern rhyme, "gooþ," pr. pl. 760. There are also several examples of OE. *y*, *ȳ* in rhyme with OE. *e*, *æ*, viz. vnknitti[th] 101, mynde 165, 243, 648, felth 252, 382, 502, kynde 642, 917 (possibly a mistake for "hende," which is found in four other MSS.) ; others probably existed in 544 (see Note) and 839 (see above). The only example of OE. *i* rhyming with *e* is "telth," 384, 500, which may well be influenced by the vowel of ME. tele, OE. teolian = tilian. In this case it seems more probable that the *e*, *y* rhymes are marks of a south-eastern influence on the dialect than that they are due to a sporadic change of *i*, *y*, into *e*.

Authorship.—The opening verses of R attribute the authorship to Richard Maydenstoon (see Note 1), who was born at Maidstone, and became Bachelor and Doctor of Divinity at Oxford, dying at Aylesford in 1396. He was a theological writer of note, the confessor of John of Gaunt, and the reputed author of a collection of Latin sermons, *Sermones dormi secure*. Although one must not lay too much weight on the statement in R, the East Midland dialect with its occasional south-eastern rhymes is just what might be expected from an ecclesiastic of Kentish origin, who was mainly connected with Oxford and the Court. A striking parallel between these

Psalms and the *Sermones dormi secure* is pointed out in the note on
571-2. On the other hand, the symbolism of the sparrow, 601-4,
is different, the 21st Sermon explaining this verse to mean that the
sparrow watches her nest lest the sparrow-hawk should take her
young. 245-6 is paralleled in the *Sermones,* as in many other
medieval writings: "Nihil certius morte et nihil incertius hora
mortis. Unde.ait poeta, Hoc scio quod moriar vbi quando nescio."
This does not appear to be Latin poetry; can it conceivably be a
translation of these lines, and is the preacher referring to himself?
It is, of course, very common, cp. *Parlement of the Thre Ages,*

> "Ne noghte es sekire to ʒoure self in certayne bot dethe,
> And he es so vncertayne that sodaynly he comes,"
>
> 11.635-6;

and, later, Dunbar's *Testament of Mr. Andro Kennedy,*

> "Cum nichill sit certius morte . . .
> Nescimus quando, vel qua sorte."

A second version of the Penitential Psalms is that ascribed to
Thomas Brampton, and dated 1402, edited in Vol. 7 of the Pub-
lications of the Percy Society. It is much more definitely ecclesiastical
in tone, laying great stress on the necessity of penance, bringing out
by force of contrast the purely devotional character of the present
version. Compare, for example, stanza 17 with the corresponding
stanza in Brampton, v. 22 :

> "ʒyf thou, with good avysement,
> Of thi synnes wilt the schryve,
> Thi soule in helle schal nevere be schent
> Whil thou wilt here thi penaunce dryve,"

or stanza 101 with Brampton, v. 106 :

> "A *law of mercy* thou hast gyven
> To hym that wyll no synnes hyde,
> But clenly to a preest be schryven."

In v. 59 Brampton states the doctrine of the Immaculate Conception
(cp. stanza 54 in our version) :

> "Of my modyr I was conceyved
> In synne, and so was every chylde
> (After that Adam was dysceyved)
> Sauf Cryist alone and Marie mylde."

Another typical passage is v. 48 :

> "Here no lengere taryen I may,
> In erthe I schal no lengere dwelle ;
> Harde peynes I muste assay,
> In purgatorye, or ellys in helle."

Brampton is also concerned with the duties of knights, kings, with mention of

> "oure kyng, be trewe fay,
> That schal heretykes alle distrye,"

and priests (vv. 87–96). The only point of contact between the two versions, beyond commonplace phrases like v. 55, "And lese noȝt that thou hast bowȝt" (cp. 24), is quoted in the Note to 361–8.

V. Lessons from the Dirige.—This piece consists of the Lessons of the Dirige, *i. e.* Matins of the Office for the Dead, with the Responsories and Versicles, and the Canticle of the Last Judgment which concludes the Office, following the Use of Sarum. The Office itself is found in English in the *Prymer*, ed. Littlehales, E.E.T.S. 105, pp. 56–70, and in Maskell's *Monumenta Ritualia*, Vol. III (in both of which, it may be noted in passing, the translation of the Lessons is taken from Purvey's revision of the first Wycliffite Bible), and in Latin in the *Sarum Breviary*, ed. Procter and Wordsworth, Vol. II, pp. 274–9. Our version is the same as that found in an English MS. Primer in the British Museum, Add. 27592, the notice of which in the Catalogue states that it differs from that printed by Maskell, and agrees more with Camb. Univ. MS. Dd. xi. 82, and Bodleian Douce MSS. 246, 275. The translator used a Latin Primer, with the help of Purvey's text. As a rule, he retained Purvey's vocabulary, but brought the order of the words much closer to the Latin, *e.g.* wheþer as dayes of men þi dayes, 60/9 ; for I haue no wickid þing doon, 60/11–12 ; and similarly in the Versicles and Responses the Latin order is preserved, *e.g.* my trespasse I dreede, and bifore þee I am a-schamyed, 60/32, cp. *Prymer*, p. 60. In a very few cases this practice leads him into pedantry, as in 61/20 and 63/7, but as a rule it only imparts a poetical character to his style. In many cases he substitutes a simpler English word for a Romance word in Purvey, *e.g.* "heuy" for "greuouse," 59/9 ; "seeke" for "enquere," 60/10 ; "ransake" (Norse) for "enserche," 60/11 ; "schopyn" for "formed," 60/21 ; "goost" for "spirit," 60/28. Several of these, as the first two quoted, are found in the earlier text of Hereford, but this is natural, and probably due to coincidence. Where he varies from Purvey in sense, it is for the worse, as in his translations of *Job* xvii. 14, 62/29–31, and his rendering of *mercenarii* as "of a merchant," 61/30, and of *os* as "mouth," 63/7. Both these latter are of course possible, but the sense is not to be com mended. His rendering of *immutatio* as "goostly liknesse," 62/8, points to a variant reading *imitatio*, and testifies to his careful use of his sources. It should also be recorded that the translator of the *Prymer*, who follows Purvey very closely, was not entrapped by *Job* xvii. 15, where the text of the Office differs from that of the *Vulgate*.

Two verse paraphrases of the Lessons are edited by Dr. Kail, E.E.T.S. 124 (*Twenty-six Political and other Poems*). Of these the second, *Pety Job*, is a paraphrase, verse by verse, of the nine Lessons, a twelve-line stanza to each verse. The first, called *The Lessouns of the Dirige*, is less expanded. After the first two lessons, it includes the Responsories and sometimes the Versicles, following Sarum Use, and also the Canticle of Judgment. A comparison of the language shows that it is, except in a few important points, founded on our version; *cp.* for example, *Lessons* 33-62 with 60/2–13. Again, the same mistranslation of *Job* xvii. 14 is found in both, and other parallels are recorded in the Notes. Its author's use of the Latin, however, is shown by his correct translation of *os* and *mercenarii*, his misunderstanding of *nervo*, *Job* xiii. 27, and his rendering of "goostly liknesse" as "folwyng" (see Notes).

VI. **A Song of Mercy and Judgment.**—There are three other MSS. of this poem, which is in the East Midland dialect: Harl. 1704, ed. Patterson, *The Middle English Penitential Lyric*, pp. 85-8, Lambeth 853, ed. Furnivall, E.E.T.S. 24, pp. 18–21, and Brit. Mus. Add. 31042, ed. Brunner, *Archiv* CXXXII, pp. 321–3. Of these, Lambeth is the longest, containing two verses more than our MS., of which v. 5 corresponds to Harl. v. 3, and v. 6 to Add. v. 4. The order also is different, Lambeth reversing vv. 3 and 4, and then inserting the two additional verses. In his notes, Dr. Patterson points out passages drawn from *St. Edmund's Mirror* and from the Responses in the *Dirige*. The echo in ll. 11–12 of the Canticle of Judgment (p. 64) is probably the reason for its standing next after it in the MS.

VII. **A Prayer for Mercy.**—The dialect of this is also East Midland; the strong pp. has lost -*n*; the Southern ind. pr. pl.

"askiþ" appears once, 20. Final -e is much more often syllabic
than in the previous poem.

This poem is also found in MS. Camb. Kk. 1, 6, and printed by
Dr. MacCracken in *Archiv* CXXXI, pp. 43–4, in a collection of
religious poems written under apparent Lydgatian influence. Our
poem, however, is not marked by the " aureate" language which
characterises the others.

VIII. **God's Complaint.**—Of this poem there are eight MSS. :
Bodley 596, Rawlinson C. 86, Douce 78, Trinity College, Cambridge
600 (R. 3. 20), Harleian 2380 (defective and incomplete, lacking
vv. 6, 8, 10), Lambeth 306, 853 (these two are edited by Dr.
Furnivall, E.E.T.S. 15, p. 190), and Adv. 34, 7, 3, of which stanzas
1–7, 11, 12, were printed by Laing in *Early Metrical Tales*, 1826,
pp. 299–303.

The form of the poem is based on the *Reproaches*, a part of the
Liturgy for Good Friday (see *Sarum Missale*, ed. Dickinson, p. 327),
the first three verses, and a fourth which is found in MS. Adv., also
following in subject-matter the antiphons of this service, as is shown
in the Notes.   A Southern English metrical form of the *Reproaches*,
from a MS. of 1330, is given in Wright's *Reliquiæ Antiquæ*, II, 225.

Of the Oxford MSS., Bodley, which belongs to the early fifteenth
century, is almost identical, except for its omission of l. 28, with our
text, and might be derived directly from it, but that it has the correct
reading "boght" in l. 2.   The other two are late and inferior, Douce
omitting stanzas 6 and 9, and reversing stanzas 4 and 5.

IX. **To God.**—This and the two following poems have not, as far
as I know, been printed before, nor are they found in any other MS.
There is a certain likeness in sense between this and the opening of
Richard de Castre's Prayer to Jesus (E.E.T.S. 24, p. 15).

XII. **Hymn from the "Speculum Christiani."**—This was evidently an exceedingly popular poem in the Middle Ages.   The
British Museum has ten MS. versions : Harl. 206, 1288, 2382
(edited by Patterson, *The Middle English Penitenital Lyric*, pp. 139–
41), 5396, 6580, Lansdowne 344, Royal 8. E. V., 17, A. xxvii, Add.
10052, 15237, 21202, 22121, 37787.   In addition, there are at
Oxford Laud Misc. 104, 513, Hatton 97, Ashm. 61, 750, Rawl. C.
401, Bodley 89, 61, 850, Rawl. lit. g. 2, Add. A. 268, Eng. th. e.
16 ; at Cambridge Dd. 14. 26. III, Ff. 1. 14, 5. 48 (printed in *Reliquiæ
Antiquæ* II, 212), Hh. 1. 13, Ii. 6. 43, Jesus Coll. 51 (Q.G. 3), Pem-
broke 285, St. John's Coll. 176 (G. 8), Sidney Sussex 55 ; also Trin.

Coll., Dublin 159 (C. 3. 13), Edin. Univ. Laing 32, Lambeth 559, Greg. MS., Helmingham Hall L. J. 5. 14, Petworth MS. 8, Longleat 29, and St. Cuthbert's College MS.

In perhaps the greater number of cases the poem is incorporated in a Latin manuscript of the *Speculum Christiani*. This was a popular theological treatise belonging to the second half of the fourteenth century, as Richard Rolle of Hampole is quoted under the section "De Tribus Generibus Orationum," and probably written in England, as it quotes the Lambeth Constitutions of 1281.˙ It is interspersed with some English prose and several English rhymes, which loosely paraphrase or summarise the succeeding Latin text. The amount of verse included varies in different MSS., our poem not appearing in Harl. 1197, 2250. The book is divided into eight Tabulæ, the eighth of which consists of a prayer for the Elevation, two hymns to the Blessed Virgin, and two ladders leading to Heaven and Hell. Our poem stands before the first of the hymns, *Gaude flore virginali*, a hymn on the Seven Joys of our Lady in Heaven ; see *Daniel Thesaurus Hymnologicus*, I, 346, *Mone, Lateinische Hymnen des Mittelalters*, Bd. II, p. 76, *Gaude virgo, mater Christi*, and an English version in E.E.T.S. 15, p. 174, "Gaude, the flowre of virginyte." It is with a verse from this hymn that Fabyan concludes each of the seven books of his *Chronicle*. The English poem can scarcely have been written as a translation of this, nor is it at all likely to be by the same hand as the rest of the verse, which, though often vigorous,[1] is very unmetrical, e. g.

> "The wise man forsothe wil nat sett his herte
> On thinge that may not longe stande in qwerte,
> But on the eende he hath mynde,
> And nothing settes before that schuld be behinde;"

which is a not unfair example of the average standard reached. It was probably inserted, for the benefit of the unlearned reader, as the most accessible representation of the Latin ; it may be noted that the latter, though it does not deal with the Five Joys, is headed "Quinque Gaudia Marie." The book was printed by Machlinia, and is described by W. Herbert in Ames's *Typographical Antiquities*, 1785, Vol. I,

---

[1] *E. g.* an interesting poem, never printed since the first edition of 1480, on the magnificence of Jerusalem, and its destruction as God's punishment of the covetousness of the Jews. The fire of covetousness, says the poet, still throws up so great a smoke that nearly all men of high rank are blear-eyed or blind (B.M. Add. 15237, 27b–28b).

1,13, where the poem is printed. In the later editions these English elements do not appear.

In the Vernon Manuscript, however, which is dated at about 1385, there is a poem which is simply an expanded form of the present one, each line being lengthened to six feet, and the same rhymes being kept (ed. Horstmann, E.E.T.S. 98, 22). It is interesting to notice that it agrees with our text against the version in the MSS. and printed text of the *Speculum* in 10–14, 35–8, 43–4, 51–2, as may be seen by comparing with Dr. Patterson's text. In addition, MSS. Royal 17 A. xxvii., B.M. Add. 37787, Lambeth 559, Rawl. liturg. g. 2, which are all unattached to the *Speculum*, give our version. Ashmole 61, alone of the Oxford and London MSS., though detached from the *Speculum*, shows a blending of both types. It is dated by Horstmann as in or before the time of Henry VII. It seems therefore most probable that the present text represents the original form of the poem.

In Myrc's *Duties of a Parish Priest* (ed. Peacock, E.E.T.S. 31), there seems to be a reminiscence of our poem in ll. 290–301.

XIII. **Life of Adam and Eve.**—Other MSS. of this version are : British Museum Harl. 4775 (H, printed *Archiv* 74, p. 353), Harl. 1704 (H$_2$), Harl. 2388 (H$_3$), Egerton 276 (E), Oxford Bodl. 596 (B, printed *Archiv* 74, p. 345), Douce 15 (D), Douce 372 (D$_2$), Ashmole 802 (A), Lambeth 72 (L). Other versions are: MS. Auchinleck (Au, ed. Horstmann, *Sammlung Altenglischer Legenden*, 1878, p. 139), *Canticum de Creatione* (C, *ib.* p. 124), MS. Vernon (V, *ib.*, p. 220). The sources of our version are : (1) the Latin *Vita Adae et Evae*, (2) a Latin account of the traditional derivation of Adam's name, and of the materials of which his body was made, (3) connecting parts of the Bible narrative to make this into a continuous story.

(1) The legendary history of Adam and Eve, their penance in the waters of Jordan and Tigris, the journey of Eve and Seth to the gates of Paradise, and the death and burial of Adam, with the account of the tables written by Seth, are derived from the *Vita Adae et Evae* (ed. W. Meyer, *Königliche Bayerische Akademie der Wissenschaften, Abhandlungen der philosophisch-philologische Classe*, Bd. 14, Abtheilung 3, pp. 187–250, 1878). This, together with the Greek *Apocalypse of Moses* (ed. Tischendorf, *Apocalypses Apocryphae*, 1866), represents an original Jewish Book of Adam. Both are translated and edited by Wells in Archdeacon Charles's *Apocrypha and Pseudepigrapha of the Old Testament*, II, 123–54.

According to Meyer, the *Vita* is later than the Latin text of the *Gospel of Nicodemus*, i.e. than the third or fourth century A.D. The MSS. can be divided into three classes : I, from which the standard text is taken ; II, which was in existence about the year 730, and which has two passages not found in I, namely 90/24, "Also I vndirstood"—91/23, "God her iuge," and 98/14, "Thanne Seeth"—"spaken proudly" 99/10 ; and III, which has the first only of these additions, but which has four interpolations from the Legend of the Rood.

There are many additions to the text of the *Vita* in this and other English renderings, which are found in several Latin MSS. in the British Museum (Royal 8. F. xvi. 2, Harl. 275, 526, 2432, Arundel 326) ; for example, the statement that Adam and Eve, on leaving Paradise, went into the west, that Adam's long hair floated on the water, that his voice grew hoarse with his cries, that Eve, on coming out of the water, lay as dead for almost a day. But none of these represent the original from which our version was translated, as may be seen from the notes on Adam's vision and prophecy. All are very similar, except that Arundel 326 has two interpolations, telling how Seth, looking into Paradise, saw on the summit of a tree a Virgin seated, holding a crucified Child, and how Adam, hearing this, prophesied of the Virgin Birth and of the Crucifixion. Another MS., Harl. 495, is of quite a different type, sharing none of the readings characteristic of the others, but more resembling the printed text. It is incomplete, beginning with Adam's penance in Jordan, and has no *Corpus Adae*.

(2) The Latin original of the passage describing Adam's name and the making of his body, though not forming a part of the *Vita* itself, is found following it in the Latin MSS. above-mentioned, except that in Arundel 326 the last part is missing, the MS. being incomplete. The translation is literal, except that in the Latin the order is reversed, the making of Adam's body being placed first, and then the finding of his name. The MSS. also do not give the Latin verse, which is, however, found in Harl. 956 (a longer and fuller account, followed by Jean d'Outremeuse in *Ly Myreur des Histors*), where the clauses are in a different order, and the seventh and eighth are slightly different.

The derivation of Adam's name from four Greek words evidently comes from a Hellenized Jewish source. It makes its first appearance in literature in the Slavonic *Book of the Secrets of Enoch*, xxx. 13–14

(Charles, *Apocrypha*, etc., II, 449) : "And I appointed him a name, from the four component parts ; from east, from west, from south, from north. And I appointed for him four special stars, and I called his name Adam." The book is dated by Dr. Charles at about the beginning of the Christian era, the place of its composition being Egypt, and its author or final editor being a Hellenistic Jew. The derivation is given in full in the anonymous *De Montibus Sina et Sion*, 4 (Migne, *Patrologia*, IV. 912), formerly attributed to St. Cyprian, where the names of the points of the compass are taken as being those of the stars : Invenimus in Scripturis per singulos cardines orbis terrae esse a Conditore mundi quatuor stellas constitutas in singulis cardinibus. Prima stella, orientalis, dicitur a ἀνατολή, etc. So also in the Commentary on the New Testament ascribed to St. Jerome (Works, ed. Marcianaeus, 1706, Vol. V, p. 847) : Adam à quatuor literis, & à quatuor stellis nomen accepit, quod est, etc., and in the O.E. prose *Salomon and Saturn* (ed. Kemble, pp, 178, 180). For other accounts, where the stars are not confused with points of the compass, see the *Sibylline Oracles*, III, 24–6, St. Augustine, *In Joannis Evangelium Tractatus* IX, § 14, Ven. Bede, *In Genesim Expositio* IV.

The account of the different components of Adam's body also appears first in the *Book of the Secrets of Enoch*, xxx. 8 : On the sixth day I commanded my wisdom to create man from seven consistencies : one, his flesh from the earth ; two, his blood from the dew ; three, his eyes from the sun : four, his bones from stones ; five, his intelligence from the swiftness of the angels and from clouds ; six, his veins and his hair from the grass of the earth ; seven, his spirit from my breath and from the wind.

It will be seen that the differences between this and our account are that (6) in *Enoch* disappears, and that (7) becomes the fifth, seventh, and eighth parts in our version—his breath from the wind, his understanding from the light of the world, his soul from the Holy Ghost. Also, his blood is derived from the sea, not the dew, and there is no mention of the angels. The version of Jean d'Outremeuse is the same in substance, except for the curious statement that the eighth part, "qui fut de la clarteit de monde, senefie tristeure," which evidently arises from a misreading of the Latin Crist*us*, *cp.* Harl. 956, qu*od* interpretatur χρs.

The *Anglo-Saxon Ritual*, quoted by Dr. Charles, has a different account, which is also found in the prose *Salomon and Saturn*, p. 180;

the former reads as follows: Pondus limi, inde factus est caro; pondus ignis, inde rubeus est sanguis et calidus; pondus salis, inde sunt salsae lacrimae; pondus roris, inde factus est sudor; pondus floris, inde est varietas oculorum; pondus nubis, inde est instabilitas mentium; pondus venti, inde est anhela frigida; pondus gratiae, inde est sensus hominis.

This has diverged a long way from *Enoch*, and it will be noted that, with the exception of the making of man's breath from the wind, none of the divergences are shared by our version. *Salomon and Saturn*, however, has in common with our version the fact that the naming of Adam stands before the making of his body; everywhere else the order is reversed. The connection of the two can scarcely be original; the story of the naming tells us that Adam was made of earth brought from the four ends of the world. According to Rabbinical tradition, it was of different colours, red, black, white and green (Rabbi Eliezer, ed. Friedländer, p. 76). Targ. Jonathan, *Genesis* ii. 7, says: "And he took earth from the place of the Holy Temple and from the four ends of the world." Hence probably follows the Christian legend that Adam was made at Bethlehem.

(3) The connecting narrative from *Genesis* follows the earlier Wycliffite text of Hereford, c. 1382, with the exception of the introductory extract, the earlier account of the creation of Man, i. 26–31, which is taken from Purvey's revised edition of c. 1388. It is immediately followed by the second account (*Genesis* ii. 7) from the earlier text, and thus evidently represents an afterthought. We may safely infer that the present text was constructed from a Latin source combined with the English Bible, some time after 1382, and expanded at a later date, after 1388. D prefixes *Gen.* i. 1—ii. 3 from the Purveyite version, headed "Here bigynneþ þe making of [heuen] & e[rþe]." H_2, an incomplete MS. containing the beginning and end of this text, has the same structure. The intermediate portion is added in a later hand from a source closely resembling B, with no interpolations from the Bible.

This was by no means the first time that the *Corpus Adae*, the *Vita*, and *Genesis* had been combined. Meyer notes that in Cod. germ. Monac. 3866 three chapters of the *Vulgate* precede the *Vita*, *i.e.* the story is brought up from the beginning to the expulsion from Paradise, and another piece is interpolated after the *Vita's* brief mention of the slaying of Abel. Except for the *Corpus Adae*, this must cover the same ground as our present text. Jean d'Outremeuse (1338–1400) in *Ly Myreur des Histors*, Vol. I, pp. 308–24 (ed. Borgnet, Bruxelles, 1864), where the story is related in order to explain the genealogy of St. Joseph, combines a different form of the *Corpus* (the Latin of which is found in MS. Harl. 956, F. 103), which he gives on the authority of St. Jerome, with the *Vita* and the story of Cain and Abel rendered freely after the Bible. There are also other English forms of the story which must now be considered in detail.

In MS. Au there are two fragments of a life of Adam and Eve, edited by Horstmann, *Altenglische Legenden*, 1878, pp. 139–47, dated by Bachmann (*Die beiden Versionen des me. Canticum de Creatione*, Hamburg, 1891), 1300–25, and located in the North-East Midlands. The opening is lost, so that we cannot tell whether the *Corpus Adae* was already connected with it; the *Vita* proper is preceded by an account of the fall of Satan (Liȝtbern), freely as he tells it in the Vita, and the temptation and fall of man, freely from Genesis. The details mentioned above as not occurring in the printed *Vita* are not found here. The statement that it was in the *face* that the serpent bit Seth, though not in the *Vita*, is not one of these, as it arises from a scribal error due to confusion between *faciens* and *faciem;* see Bachmann, p. 48. The fragment breaks off before the birth of Cain, and the second begins in the middle of a very brief account of Adam's vision, related not to Seth alone, but to all his children, omitting his prophecy, and combined with his description of the Fall and its consequences. Many characteristic elements are omitted, *e.g.* the names of the ointments that Eve and Seth brought, the burial of Adam and Abel *in Paradise* (no place of burial being here mentioned), Eve's prophecy of the two judgments by fire and water, the guiding of Seth's hand by an angel, and the naming of the letters by Solomon. The poem concludes with a short account of O.T. judgments on sin, the Flood, the destruction of Sodom and Gomorrah, the repentance of Nineveh. It appears to be based on a MS. of the *Vita* intermediate between I and II. Specially noteworthy is the fact that it omits the name of the river (Jordan) in which Adam did penance; this is said to be a Christian substitution for one of the rivers of Paradise, see *Jewish Enclyclopedia* under "Adam." Here it is simply "þe flom," ll. 215, 237.

In the same volume, p. 220, Horstmann has published a prose life of Adam and Eve from the Vernon MS., f. 393 (denoted by V)

This was originally a poem in long lines; for example, p. 223, 14–8 can be read, by slightly altering the order of the words within the lines :

> "So þat Jhesu Crist þi penaunce haþ vnderfonge(n),
> For þou wold so bleþeliche dwelle þer-in so longe.
> I am set to bringe ʒow þer ʒe schul haue mete,
> Such as in paradys ʒe weore wont to hauc & eete(n)."
> þe corsud angel nom Eue vp bi þe hond
> & ladde hire . . . to druʒe londe ;
> As soone as Eue comen vp of þe water was,
> Hire bodi . . . was grene as eni gras.

See also 221, 1–2, 40–1; 222, 13–4, 16–7; 223, 7–9; 224, 36–7; 225, 27–8, 34–5; 226, 14–5, 38–9, etc. In many passages, however, it is not at all easy to restore the verse form without extensive alterations; there must therefore have been a long period of corruption. The MS. dates from about 1385 (Carleton Brown, *Register of Middle English Religious Verse*, 1916), the original probably belongs to the beginning of the fourteenth century, and the metre much resembles that of the Southern Legendary.

The rendering of the *Vita* which we have here closely resembles that in Au ; here again the details from the Latin MSS. do not appear. There are many omissions, such as the vision and prophecy of Adam, also passages after p. 222, 42, p. 223, 32. Two legendary additions appear, the thunder-clap at the begetting of Cain (p. 223, 37), and the Divine institution of tithe (p. 224, 15). There are also additions from the Legend of the Rood (E.E.T.S. 46, p. 19 ; 87, p. 1). In this story Adam sends Seth to Paradise for the oil of mercy, directing him to follow the track left by the footsteps of himself and Eve. Seth sees a vision through the gates of Paradise and is given by an angel three kernels of an apple, which he places under Adam's tongue when he is dead. Adam is buried in Hebron, and henceforth the legend traces the story of the rods which grew from the kernels. In the Vernon text Seth and Eve go, as in the *Vita*, but Seth is given directions as in the Legend, though they are here unnecessary. The vision is omitted, there being only a few lines describing the beauties of Paradise, we are told of the kernels, and of the burial of Adam and Abel by the angels in Hebron. Two lines (rhyming) connect the kernels with the Rood. The interpolations are so short that the piece may have been written as a companion to a Rood Legend, and may even have formed a part of the Southern Legendary, providing the account of Creation and of the early life of Adam which the Rood Legend omits. In the same way, in the *Northern Homilies*, the Rood Legend (E E.T.S. 46, p. 62) is interpolated with the *Vita*, from which it takes Adam's speech to his children, St. Michael's speech to Seth at the gates of Paradise, and the burial of Adam's body by angels (in Hebron, to suit the Rood story).

As regards the connecting matter, the *Vita* is preceded, as in Au, by the fall of the angels and of man, but not, as in Au, from *Genesis*, but from a Bible narrative full of interesting legendary details, as for example of the angels that fell from heaven : "Summe astunte in þe eyr, and summe in þe eorþe. ʒif eny mon is elue Inome oþur elue Iblowe, he hit haþ of þe angelus þat fellen out of heuene." Other additions are an account of the murder of Abel, of the begetting of Seth by Divine command, and of the inter-marriage between the children of Seth and of Cain. At the beginning is an account of creation and of the naming of Adam. The stars are here correctly given, as in MS. Harl. 956 and in Jean d'Outremeuse.

The *Canticum de Creatione* (denoted by C), edited by Horstmann in the same volume, pp. 124–38, brings us to a much later date, as the poem itself states that it was written in 1375. There is no *Corpus Adae*, and no interpolated Biblical matter beyond a very short intro-duction describing the Fall of man, and five stanzas telling of Cain's jealousy of Abel, and of the begetting of Seth. These two items, which are also in V, are found in *Cursor Mundi*, 1059–65, 1190–1218, E.E.T.S. 57, etc. Its Latin source is not the same as that of the previous poems, but seems to be identical with that of our own version, including the details derived from the Latin MSS. There are, however, two important exceptions : there is no vision or prophecy of Adam, and it is interpolated with the Legend of the Rood. Presumably it was translated from a MS. in which the Vision was accidentally omitted. In the part unaffected by the Legend there are two additions to the *Vita* text : (1) the institution of tithe by the command of an angel who appears when Satan vanishes after- the second temptation (it occurs also in V, but there it is ordered by God himself when Adam is taught to till and sow, a much more probable occasion) ; (2) the story that Eve, when she found that the devil had beguiled her twice, covered her head with a white veil, hence all women cover their heads.

The interpolation with the Rood Legend begins at l. 619, where Adam, as in V, directs Seth how to find the way to Paradise, though its independence of V, and of V's source, is shown by l. 640, "And al to-bot Seth in þe face." We also have the vision of Seth at the gates of Paradise, and the gift of the kernels. As a result of the incorporation of the Rood Legend, it was impossible, as in V, to keep the burial of Adam in Paradise, consequently he is buried in Hebron by Seth alone. The prophecy of Eve and the making of the tables by Seth and their finding by Solomon are related, and then the Rood Legend is continued.

Hence this poem is quite independent of the earlier versions, being translated from a different and later Latin version of the *Vita*, and not following the legendary additions of V, except where they are also found in *Cursor Mundi*, and probably in several other places. Its aim was not to supplement the *Legend of the Rood*, but to combine it and the *Vita* into one story. Hence it wastes very little space on Adam's history before the beginning of the *Vita*, or on the story of Cain and Abel.

There remain two printed versions in prose, printed by Horstmann in *Archiv*, Bd. 74, 1885; the first, p. 345, from MS. Bodl. 596, is denoted by B, and the second, p. 353, from MS. Harl. 4775, where it is appended to the *Golden Legend*, by H. The second is practically identical with our version, the first contains only the *Corpus Adae* and the *Vita*. In many passages the language is so similar that it is impossible that the two versions can be derived from independent translations even of the same Latin text, e. g. the *Corpus Adae* and 81/1-17; in others they are evidently derived from different Latin texts, see Note on 81/32-4. B's readings are always the better. It gives the fuller account of Eve's dream : "I saw in my slepe that Caym w*ith* his hondes arered bloode of Abel and deuoured it with his mouthe." In the vision of Adam (88/39—89/1), where there has been confusion between "currum" and "choros," it omits the chariot, and in 90/11-13, where similarly confusion between "locum" and "lacum" has caused the repetition of a sentence in H, it is correct (see Notes).

The second version (H) stands in very close connection with the present version (W), E (incomplete, extending to "dou*n*," 92/12 only), L, H$_2$, H$_3$, D, D$_2$. All of these omit "ponyschid," 97/19, and "lest" 80/17. In four of these, H, E, L, and D$_2$, the story is attached to the end of the *Golden Legend*, forming one of the additional legends which appear in the English versions only (*Legenda Aurea—Légende Dorée—Golden Legend*, by Pierce Butler, Baltimore,

1899, p. 69).[1] H₂ and D, as stated above, prefix the Purveyite version of *Genesis* i. 1—ii. 3, and then begin the ordinary text, hence repeating i. 26–31. This is evidently a later addition. The intermediate pages of H₂ are supplied in a later hand from a text very like B; they comprise the part of the text (without the Biblical additions) from "forþ," 77/13, to "beynge," 85/4. The same hand has altered "in the vale of ebron," the place of Adam's making, to "In the same place that J[hesu] was borne in, that is to seye in the Cytie of bethlem, which is in the middle of the earth," also from the B-text. E and L are both found in MSS. of the *Golden Legend*, the former following on the Advent discourse, and breaking off at "falle doun," 92/12, and L following the Concepcio Marie, and followed by "5 Willes of Pharo," and "3 Kinges of Collin." H₃ is the nearest to W, but has more scribal omissions. Neither is derived directly from the other.

W is on the whole the best of this group of texts. It alone agrees with the Latin originals in stating that Adam was made in Bethlehem and buried in Paradise. In the other texts the scene is Hebron, and in the second case they add: "as the maister of stories tellith," *i.e.* Petrus Comestor, see his *Genesis*, cap. xxiv. The *Cursor Mundi*, which knows nothing of the *Vita*, gives the Hebron story (ll. 9397, 1416), as do V and C as regards the burial; A mentions no place, but says that Eve was buried with Adam. The influence of the Rood Legend would make the burial in Paradise impossible, and hence facilitate both alterations. Only B, which is founded on a less corrupt Latin text, keeps Bethlehem and Paradise as the sites.

Other points in which W offers a better text than H are as follows: 76/26 "þo" for "ȝe," so all other MSS.; 77/6 "Geon" for "Seon," so all others; 79/32 "soule hauers" for "soulis heiris," so E, H₃; L "soulis of heuen"; 80/17 "put" for "puttith," so E, H₃; L "puttith"; 81/20 "Oure Lord God delyueride mete to beestis but to us he delyueride mete of aungels" for "Oure lorde god deliuerid vs mete of aungellis," so all others; 81/33 "suffre as manye and" for "suffre and," so H₃, E; L "suffre and"; 86/14 "hir

---

[1] The note at the end of the "Wiles of Pharao" in D₂ : "Here endith the v. wilis of kinge Pharao . . . and also here endith the lives of Seintis that is callid . . . the gilte legende . . . and here endith the life of Adam and Eve" shows the process of accretion; similarly, in MS. Balliol College 228, a fifteenth-century Latin *Golden Legend*, the *Vita* follows, though separated from the *Golden Legend* proper by a blank page, and not mentioned in the Table of Contents.

brest " for " the brest," so all others ; 87/36 " va~aunt" for " but be
vacaunt," so all others; 88/34 "inwardly " for "in worde," so all
others; 89/20 " conuerte " for "comforté," so H_3 ; H_2, E, L as H ;
90/2 " whanne " for " whom " ; H_2, H_3 " whā " ; E, L " whom "; 91/8
" saaf " for " faire," so all others ; 99/15 " hem" for "hym," so H_3 ;
H_2, L " hym."

Several times H tries to remedy obscurities caused by errors in
the MS. from which the scribe copied ; see Notes on 78/5, 10, 85/13,
87/36, 95/16.   In 88/34 and 91/17 he has misunderstood the
correct reading ; see Notes.

In the vision and prophecy of Adam the text is particularly
confused, and several passages bear witness to marginal corrections
becoming incorporated in the text alongside the passages they were
meant to correct ; see Notes on 88/39, 90/13, 28, 91/9.   In every
case B has only one of these ; in the first and last it has the corrupted text (taking the printed *Vita* as the standard), in the other
two it follows the older version.   Otherwise the MSS. all agree.

Nearly all the rubrics are peculiar to W, other MSS. only having
those on 80/24, 82/20, and 87/13.

The latest MS. of *Adam and Eve* which I have seen is MS.
Ashmole 802 (denoted by A), f. 19–48, in a collection of Dr. Simon
Forman's papers, and signed "forman 1592." Though it contains
many additions and accretions, yet where it deals with the original
matter it is nearer to our text than any of the others (see Notes on
77/27, 92/10, 96/8, 16, 31). Especially from the first of these, we may
conclude that it is actually descended from our text, although it omits
the rubrics peculiar to it.   It has much additional astrological and
legendary matter, and there are two accounts of the composition of
man's body, the first being " of red earth, of the slyme of the earth,
and of the Quintessentialle substaunce or Beste *parte* of the 4
elements." After 87/9 we are told how, except at Cain's birth, Eve
always brought forth twins, a son and daughter who married together
(see Note), and after 93/8 the 70 diseases are enumerated.   From
this point the story is influenced by the Rood Legend.   Adam sends
Seth alone to Paradise, and directs him by the path he and Eve had
made.   Eve offers to go with him lest he should lose the way.
Adam says that " when he is at the valle of Josophate he hath
but 40 daies Jornaye to parradise but goe thou alsoe."   The
angel gives Seth a branch of the Tree of Knowledge to plant on the
Mount of Lebanon, " and when that tree doth beare fruite thy father

schal be made hoole," and prophesies of Christ's coming.   The Rood
Legend is continued to the story of the Cross of Christ.

XIV. **A Prayer at the Elevation.**—This is a translation of a
Latin Eucharistic Rhythm given by Daniel, *Thesaurus Hymnologicus*,
II, 32 , and Levis, *Anecdota Sacra*, p. 107, from a missal in the
monastery at Novalesa.   The translation is almost literal, save that
" haue mercy of us " is not represented in the Latin.

The Wheatley Manuscript.

I

[AN ORISON ON THE PASSION]

(1)

I Hesu þat haste me dere bought,
   Write now gostely in my thought,
That I may with deuocion
Thynk apon thy passion.

F. 1.
Jesu, write
in my heart
the remem-
brance of
Thy Passion.

(2)

For, if my hert be hard as stoon,   5
Yhit may thow goostely write þeroon
With nayles and with speer[e] kene,
And so shul the letters wele be sene.

(3)

Write in my hert thy speches swete
Whan Iudas þe traytour can þe mete ;   10
That traytour was ful of þe feende,
And ȝit thow callyd hym thy freende.

Thou didst
call Judas
Thy friend ;
how sweet
will be Thy
speech to
Thy true
friends in
Heaven !

(4)

Swete Ihesu, how myght thow soo
Calle thi freende so felle a fo ?
Bot, sithen þou spaak so louely   15
To hym þat was þine enemy,

(5)

How swete shal þi speche be
To them þat hertly louen the
Whan they in heuene with þe shul duelle
Forsothe þer may no tonge telle.   20

(6)

F. 1*b*.

Write how þow were bounden sore

Write in my
heart how
Thou wert
tried and
condemned ;

And drawen forth Pylat byfore,

How swetely þou answerde þoo

To hym þat was thi felle foo.

(7)

Write how þat fals enquest   25
Cried ay with-outen rest :
" Hong hym on the roode tree,
For he wil kyng of Iewes be."

(8)

Write vpon myne hert[e] booke
Thy fayre and thi rewely looke,   30
For schame of ther hydouse crye
þat walden of þe haue no mercy.

(9)

How Thou
barest Thy
Cross ;

Write, whanne þe crosse was forth broght,
And þe nayles of yren wroght,
How þow began to chyuer and quake,   35
Thi hert was woo if þou noght spaak.

(10)

Write how douneward þou can loke
Whan Iewes to þe þe crosse betook ;
Thow bare it forth with rewly chere,
The teres ran doune by thy lere.   40

(11)

F. 2.

Ihesu, write in my hert depe
How þat þow began to wepe

How Thou
wert nailed
to the Cross;

Whan þi baak to þe rode was [b]ent,
With rugged nayles thi handes rent.

(12)

Write þe strokes of hameres stoute,   45
With þe bloode rennyng al aboute,
How the nayles stynten at the boone
Whan thow were ful woo-bygone.

43. MS. lent.

(13)

Ihesu, write ȝit in myne hert
How bloode oute of þi woundes stert ;   50
And with þi blood write thow so oft
In myne hert to hit be soft.

(14)

Ihesu, þat art so mykel of myght,
Write in myne hert þat rewful syght,   Of Thy grief
                                               in looking
To loke on thi moder fre   55   on Thy
                                               Mother;
Whan þou were honged on roode tre.

(15)

Write thi swete modres woo
Whan sche sawe [the] to deeth[e] goo ;
I-wys if I write al my lyue
I schuld neuer here woo dyscryue ;   60
In myne hert ay mote hit be,   F. 2b.
That harde knotty roode tre,—   And of all
                                       the attri-
                                       butes of Thy
(16)   Passion.

The nayles and the spere also
That thow were with to deth[e] doo,
The croune and þe scourges grete   65
That thow was with so sore bete,

(17)

Thi wepyng and thi woundes wyde,
The bloode þat ran doun by þi syde,
The schame and scorne and grete dispite,
The spatil þat foulid þi face white,   70

(18)

The eysell and þe bettir galle,
And other of thi peynes alle ;
For, whiles I haue them in my thought,
The deuyl, I hope, sal dere me nought.

(19)

Ihesu, write þus, þat I may knowe   75   Grant me to
                                                       know what
How mykel loue to the I owe,   Thou hast
                                                       done for me,
For, if þat I wil from the fle,   and how I
                                                       should love
Thow folowest ay to saue me.   Thee.

(20)

Ihesu, whan I thenk on the,
How þou was bounden for loue of me,　　　　80
Wele ought I to wepe þat stounde
þat þow so sore for me was bounde.

F. 3.

(21)

Bot thow þat bare vpon thin handes
For my synnes so bytter bandes,
With loue bondes bynde thow so me　　　　85
þat I neuer depart from the.

(22)

Ihesu, þat was with loue so bounde,
þat suffred for me dedes wounde,
At my dying visite me,
And make the feend away to fle.　　　　90

Be with me at my death.

(23)

Ihesu, make me glad to be
Symple and poure for loue of the,
And lat me neuer for more ne lasse
Loue good to mykil þat sone sal passe.

Teach me to love Thee above all transitory good.

(24)

Ihesu, þat art kyng of lyfe,　　　　95
Teche my soule, þat is thi wyfe,
To loue best no thing in londe
Bot the, Ihesu, here dere housebonde.

(25)

For othir joye and othir blys,
Wo and sorow forsothe it is,　　　　100
And lastis but a litil while,
Mannes soule for to bygyle.

F. 3*b*.

(26)

Lat me fele what ioye it be
To suffre woo for loue of the,
How myry it is for the to wepe,　　　　105
How soft in harde clothes to slepe.

Let me rejoice to suffer for Thee.

98. MS. *adds:* For othir blys and othir bewte
Is bot foule and sorow to se.

(27)

Lat now loue his bowe bende
And loue-arowes to my hert sende,
That they peers[e] to the rote,
For swilk woundes schuld be my bote.   110

(28)

When I am lowe for thi loue,
Than am I moost at myne aboue,
Fastyng is feest, mornyng is blys,
For thi loue pouert is ryches ;

(29)

The hard heyre schuld be more of pryse   115
þanne soft sylk or pelour or byse,
Defaute for thy loue is plente,
And fleschely lust ful loth schuld be.

(30)

Whanne I am with woo bystad,   F. 4.
For thi loue thanne am I glad ;   120
To suffre scornes and greet dispite
For loue of the is my delyte.

(31)

Ihesu, make me on nyght to wake   May I think
And in my thought thi name to take,   of Thee in
And, whethir the nyght be schort or longe,   125
Of the, Ihesu, ay be my song,

the night,
and draw
Thee into
my heart by
the chain of
prayer.

(32)

And this preyer a cheyn[e] be
To drawe the doun of thi see,
That thow may make þe a duellyng
At myn hert at thi lykyng.   130

(33)

Ihesu, I pray, forsake nought me   Thou Who
Gyf I of synne gylty be,   forgavest
For to þat theef þat honge the by
Redily þow gaue hym þi mercy.

the penitent
thief, for-
sake me not
when I fall
into sin.

(34)

Ihesu, þat greet curtasye   135
Maketh me bolde on the to crye,
For wele I woot with-outen drede
Thi mercy is more þanne my mysdede.

(35)

F. 4b.

Ihesu, þat art soo leue and dere,
Here and spede this poure preyer ;   140

Thou Who didst not forsake St. Paul, though he never prayed to Thee,

For Paule, tha[t] was so fell and woode
To spille Cristen mennes blode,
To the wolde he no preyer make,
And ȝit thow wolde hym nought forsake.

(36)

Be with me when I die, that I may live with Thee.

Thanne may þow noght forsake me,   145
Sithen þat I preye thus to the ;
At my dying I hoope i-wys
Of thy presence shal I not mys.

(37)

Ihesu, make me thanne to ryse
Fro deeth to lyue on swiche wyse   150
Os thow roos on Estre Day,
In joye and blys to lyue for ay.   Amen.

II

[A PRAYER TO THE BLESSED VIRGIN]

Hail, Mary, Queen of Heaven.

HAyle, bote of bale, blissed Qwene !
    To sight so semely is noon sene ;
Lady of aungels, qwene of heuen,

F. 5.

Emprice of helle is þat I [n]eue[n].
Haile Mary, modir of grete mercy,   5
To the with hart I calle and cry,

Hear me in my wretchedness.

On hast thow here þis wrecched thing
That maketh to the this pure pra[i]yng ;

141. MS. thas.   4. MS. mene.

For sere thynges me hath vmset,
That prey to the me wille lett ;   10
For in erthe, in welthe and woo,
Thow haue[s] þi freende and I my foo,
Þow art syker and I am in drede ;
Too deeth my synnes wil me lede,   *My sins*
And saith me it is no bote   15   *tempt me to*
Though I falle the too foote.   *despair.*

If I myne eghen vn-to the cast,
Ther-agayne my synnes er faast,
And saith me þat I doo nought ryght,
For I wrethed the with my sight   20   *I have sin-*
Whanne I behelde wantonnes   *ned with my*
                                                        sight ;
And sett my thought o[n] wykkednesse.
How schal I thanne be so boolde
The with myne eghen to be-holde,   *F. 5 b.*
That haue the wrethed wrangly,—   25
How schal I of the gete mercy ?
A ! Lady, what schal I doo
If I dar nought loke the too,   *How dare I*
                                                        look to
Or how schal I on the eghen caste   *thee ?*
That I wote to the haue trespast ?   30
Thus my synnes will me feer
For sight that I may nought for-bere ;   *I might*
But here-agayne I wend to say   *answer that,*
                                                        however I
That the, Lady, loue I ay ;   *sinned, I*
And, how soo I me mys-bare,   35   *have ever*
Ou the my troost was euer-mare.   *trusted in*
                                                        thee ;
But sone come it in-to my thought
That this answere avayleth nought,
For Ihesu thi sone hateth al synne   *But that I*
                                                        remember
And alle the folyes that men lyf inne.   40   *that thy Son*
For-why our synne that we nóght leue,   *hateth all*
                                                        sin.
It is no drede that we hym greue.   *Who can*
                                                        grieve Him,
Lady, who greueth hym and payith the ?   *and yet be*
                                                        acceptable
How schul his fomen on the see ?   *to thee ?*
For they greue hym so rightwisly,   45   *F. 6.*
And thow louyst hym so tenderly.

12. MS. haueth. I *written above the line.*   22. MS. of.

Whenne he is wrothe þou art nought blythe,
Allas, allas, that hard syth!
That may I say, allas, allas,
For now is warre thanne ere was.   50

If ye both be   Lady, I haue greued yow bothe,
against me,
who can help   And that vnto myne owen skathe.
me?
                Lady, who schal halde me fro peyne
                If [ȝ]e too halde me agayne?
                If [ȝ]e wil me saue, borowed I be,   55
                And if [ȝ]e wil nought, may non help me.

Wo to you,   A! synnes, synnes, wo yow be,
my sins; ye
have de-   For fouly haue [ȝ]e gyled me;
ceived me.
First ye   For soo ye reft me skilwys syght,
seemed
small, now   Whenne I yow wrought ye semed light,   60
ye are great.
                But whenne I w[eie]de my trespas,
                Neuer no leede so heuy was.
                Wele I wote I was a fonne
F. 6 b.   Whenne I troosted yow vpon.
                For þat I ere loghe, now I grete;   65
                Allas, I wroght yow euer yette!
                First were ye soft, and now ye prik;
                A, wist I nought ye were soo wyk!
                First were ye stille, now are ye hye;
                First ye glo[þer]ed, now ye wrye.   70

Ye have de-   My frendes haue ye made my foon;
prived me of
my friends.   To whom for help may I goon?
                Me schames to loke vp-on brade,
                And haue wrechid synnes made.

Not in sight   Wher-to for syght schuld me schame?   75
alone have I
sinned, but   I haue no lym with-outen blame.
in all my
other senses.   I wolde be blynde as any stane,
                Soo þat othir synnes hade I nane;
                But with my handes I haue done ille,
                With mouthe synned agayne skille,   80
                With heryng lyked my wantonnes
                And hirked sone to here goodnesse;
                In hert haue I halden pryde
F. 7.   Night and day many a tyde;

54, 55, 56, 58. MS. the.   59. reft *crossed out after* me.
61, MS. wolde,   70, MS. gloryed.

On flesshly lykyng haue I thought,   85
Of couatyse qwyt am I nought,
My feete to ille haue gane, I knowe,
And vn-to goodnesse been ful slawe ;
Dauid worde haue I vptane,
þat says, " In my flessh is heel nane."   90
A ! Marye qwene, of wymen floure,
Cristes modir, Goddes boure,
Neuer noo synne in the was ;
What may I praye the for my trespas ?
Alle thing þat I knawe in me   95
Is welatesom to thi sone and to the ;
My handes ar lothe, my mouthe is filde,
My wikked hert hath ben to wylde,
Alle thing þat I þere-of [t]elle
Is filed of þat foule welle.   100
Lady, whethir is better I hald me stille,
Or with my mouthe speke the vn-tille ?
Or what wille þow amendes take
For my sinnes grete and blake ?
Hert, if thow thi peril wist,   105
It were no wondir if þou woldist brest.
What goodnesse fyndist þou in synne,
That thow lyked soo ther-inne ?
Thow hast fordone thin owen state
And take to helle the euen gate,   110
Thow hast wrethed Ihesu and swete Mary ;
Therfore the aght to be sory,
For to alle in heuene art thow lothe
Whiles thoo too ar with the wrothe,
Dar noon schewe the lightsom mode   115
Whiles thei be wrothe þat be so good.
Hardely synnes haue sorowful eendes,
þat maken a man lese swich too frendes,
For more likyng is on hem to se
Than a thousand wynter in synne to be.   120
Hert of ston, wilt thow nought melt ?
For sorow me thynk the aght to swelt ;

Thou art sinless ; how dare I approach thee, who am utterly defiled?

F. 7 b.

Heart of mine, why didst thou rejoice in sin ?

Thou hast angered Jesus and Mary ; who will show thee friendship?

99. MS. helle.   113. To *written above the line.*

To the blys of heuen ther the neuer aghttil

F. 8.

Bot Ihesu and Mary wil with the saghtil.

Thou canst not gain Heaven till thou hast made peace with them.

Dry hert, thow haues hard telle   125
How Crist says in his gospell
Ilk a tre þat on rote stode
And brought forth no fruyt gode
Shal be hewen doun at the laste,
And in the fyre to brenne it schal be cast.   130

Thou art a tree that brings not forth good fruit; thou wilt be cast into hell.

A! wrecched hert, fyre bronde,
How longe on rote wenist thow to stonde?
Thi fruyte is roten and baysk for synne,
To the fyre thow moost goo to brenne
Bot Ihesu and Mary schewe ther goodnesse,   135
That thow wrethed with thi wikkednesse.

Jesu, Saviour, save me from damnation.

A! Ihesu, Ihesu, for thy grete vertu,
Schew to me thow hatte Ihesu;
For that knawes olde and [ȝ]yng,
That Ihesu is saueour of alle thyng.   140
Saue me therfore fro endles schame,
For of saueour thow berest the name;
How schal thow thin owen name tyne

F. 8b.

To put me wrecche to sorow and pyne?
Or whi schul we the Ihesu calle   145
If thow þare synful dampne alle?
My synnes er gretter than me gode ware,
Bot I wote thy mercy is wel mare.
Warne me not, Ihesu, for my mysdede;
Of thi mercy is me grete nede.   150

Mary, be my help in the Day of Judgment.

A! Mary, whanne I began my tale
Th[e] I called bote of bale.
To me this synful be thow bute
Whanne I schal to þ[at] aweful mute,
To answere of ilk dede and thought,   155
On þat dredeful day thow fail me nought.

Moses commanded that he who found a thing should return it to him who had lost it.

Lady, Moyses in the olde lawe
Wrote to the folk swich a sawe,
Who-so other mannes gode may fynde,
Thei schul nought leue it hem be-hynde,   160

139. MS. þyng.   152. MS. thanne.   154. MS. þi.

Bot to syker stede it schal be brought,
And gyuen agayn whan it were sought.
But Lady, byfore Ihesu face,
Sayde the aungel, thow hast founde grace ;
And I haue losed grace for my trespas, 165
Therfore to the I come þat funden it has.
Of thi grete grace geete me a droope,
And thool me neuer falle in wanhope.

F. 9.
Obtain for
me the grace
which thou
hast found
and I have
lost.

Lady, mankynde trowen it wole
That thow was haylsed with Gabriel 170
And glathed with the Holy Gaste
When thow conceyued God of myghtes maste.
I pray þe hartly for that grete blys
Forgyf me that I haue don amys ;
For the aungel taght the al holynes, 175
And I was egged to wikkednes.

For thy Joy
when
Gabriel
greeted
thee in holi-
ness, forgive
me, who was
tempted to
wickedness.

Sithen vmthenk the þat [þou] was fayn
When thow bare Ihesu with-oute payne,
And onely had a child, as clerkes rede,
With-outen losyng of thy maydenhede. 180
For that ioy and blys þat thow had there,
Haue pite of my rewful fare,
For I brought forth wikkednesse,
And losed al my clennes.

For thy Joy
when thou
broughtest
forth thy
Son, have
pity on me,
who brought
forth
wickedness.

Mary, who myght thy joyes telle 185
Whanne Ihesu thi sone heryid helle
And rose froo deeth on sonnes morne,
That he tholed for vs beforne?
Lady, what blys had thow thanne,
Whanne thi sone roos bothe God & man, 190
F[rom] deeth þat he tholed thare,
That thow loked on with sorow & care !
For that grete blys I the beseke
With worde of mouthe and hert meke,
Reyse me fro deeth, þat ille has wrought, 195
And bryng to Ihesu þat me dere bought.
Lady, who may wete how þou were glad,
Or telle with tong what ioye þow had,

F. 9 b.
For thy Joy
when He
rose from the
dead, raise
me from
death !

For thy Joy
when He
ascended to
Heaven, let
me not sink
to Hell.

163. *Catch-word* sayde. 183. fort *crossed out after* forth.
191. MS. for.

When thow sawe wi*th* thi bodily sight
Thi sone stegh vp wi*th* his bodily myght,   200
And sett hym on his fader right hand
To be Lorde and God alle weldant ?
Of joye, Lady, the vmbethyng,
And thole me neuer to helle doun synk
For my synnes heuy as the leede,   205
That me wil drawe to sorow steede.
Thow were glad, Lady, as telleth the boke,

Whenne thi sone Ihesu to hym the vptooke ;

Glad thow were whanne ȝe two mett,
Abouen aungels kynde there he the sett.   210
Whanne þow sittist coronde in heuene,
To the I pray with mylde steuen,
Haue pite of me in thi wel-fare,
That left is here in sorow and care.

Vmthynk the, Lady, thi sone me wrought,   215
And sithen on roode me dere bought,
Thi sone made me to his lyknesse,
Though I fyled me with wykkednesse.
For loue of thi sone visage
Haue rewthe on me, his fyled ymage ;   220
Of synne and filthe thow make me clene,
For mercyful thow art and myghty qwene.

If thow say, Lady, thi sone is wrothe,
And synne to hym hath made me lothe,
I wot wele I haue wrethed hym ille,   225
But thow may saghtil vs if þow wille.
Schew hym þi eghen þat for hym greete
Whenne he on rode þanne payed oure deet ;
Schew hym thi mouthe þat kissed hym swete

Whanne he was ȝonge and litil ȝete ;   230
Schewe hym thi pappes for my trespas,
That he soked whenne he ȝonge was ;
Schew hym thi handes þat handild hym soft,
And thi armes þat hym bare oft ;
And wele I wote saghtilde I be,   235
If þese tokynes of loue thow schewe for me.

Lady, ȝit if it be sayde
That the fader of heuene be myspayde

For my synnes þat I haue wrought
In wil, in werk, in worde and thought,   240
Pray thi sone schewe hym for me
What payne he tholed on rode tre,
And sone I hope to gete forgyfnes
Of my synnes more and les.
Lady, ther is no thing þat me may dere,   245
If thow aboute be me to wereꝉ.
Alle sary hauen ioy of thi gode fame,
To them is ioye þi blisful name ;
For wele is thi name made, swete Lady,
Of M and A, R and I.   250
M is medycyn to alle seke
Þat it wil pray with hert meke.
Thi medycyn, Lady, to me þow schewe,
For my grete sekenes wele I knowe.
To the I ȝelde me, fayr pray[ande],   255
Lat me neuer perisshe vndir þi hande.
If thow for sekenes me wil forsake,
Wil noon to hele me vndirtake.
A is autour of holynes,
Where Ihesu goodnesse offyrde is.   260
To þat auter I wil my offryng make,
If ther were any þat wolde it take ;
But the auter is ryche, þe keper is grete,
With my pore offryng wele may th[am] w[l]ete ;
But Ihesu in the gospel boke   265
Þe wedow offring to þe most thank toke,
Two mytes of a ferthing prys,
For þe maner was gode and wys.
But, swete Lady, þow me nought wyte,
I haue now a-nother myte ;   270
ꝉBody and soule ar mytes two,
Omange þi offryng thole þam goo,
And, whethir þat I wake or slepe,
On thise two mytes gyf þow kepe.
The thred lettre of thy name, Lady,   275
R, is ryuer of mercy.

pray thy Son to intercede for me.

Thy name is joy to the sorrowful:

F. 11.
M is medicine for the sick ;
Grant me that medicine.

A is the altar of holiness ;

Like the widow in the gospel, I will offer my two mites,—my body and soul.

F. 11 b.

R is the river of mercy ;

246. MS. werre.   255. MS. praying.
264. MS. thei.   271. MS. but body.

My lyf and helo is al in waght
But of þat water I haue a draght.
Lady, wha[m]e wil þow mercy bede,
If thei þat pray þe may not spede ;   280
Or, if þe wille of mercy be any tyme dry,
Who to þe for mercy wil any tyme cry ?

þerfore, Lady, schewe thi godenes,
Lat me not in þis thriste goo dryngles.

I, Lady, is þe ferthe lettre, I wote ;   285
þat wele acordes vnto þi state ;
For als iustice of lyueraunce we þe calle,
þat God hath sett to help vs alle.
þi commission is trewe and large,
þerfore to me be schelde and targe,   290
And thole neuer dome passe me agayn,
Bot saue me euer fro endles payn.
Lady, I am fayn þat þow fares wele ;
Haue reuth of my wo þat I sore fele ;
And a thyng, I pray þe, to hert þow take,   295
þat Ion þi cosyn in his book spake :
He says, " Who-so haues þe worldes gode,
And to þe nedful noght turnes his mode,
Of hym þat can I not telle
How charite in hym schalle dwelle."   300

A, Lady, what blys has þow and wel-fare !
What sorow haue I and whatkyn care !
How schuld charite in the be
Ȝif þow haue no-kyn reuthe of me ?
Lady, comly qwene of hey state,   305
þis begger mesil crieth at thi ȝate ;
Sende to me some almes dede,
Or elles I perische in sorow and nede.

Lady, þow art called my sister in þe book,
þi sone oure brother þat oure kynde took,   310
Brothir and sister, I can na mare,
But bryng me oute of my [mys]fare,
And, if ȝe brothirhede wil me warne,
Help me als a godesluf-barne.

Side notes:

Grant me to drink of it.

I is for Justice ;

Grant me a merciful judgment.

F. 12.

Remember the saying of thy cousin St. John: he who succours not the needy has not charity.

If thou succour not me, how can charity be in thee?

Thy Son is our Brother, thou art our sister.

But if ye refuse me as a true brother, yet help me as a bastard.

279. MS. whanne.

A, Lady, graunt me my bone, 315

For his loue þat made bothe sone and mone,

Þat alle þat wil þis lere or rede

Þow be þer help at her moost nede,

And forgyf hem þat haues done mys,

And bryng vs alle to þi sone blys. Amen. 320

F. 12 b.

Forthy Son's sake, grant thy help to all who read or learn this hymn.

III.

[HYMN TO ST. JOHN THE BAPTIST.]

(1)

BLissed be thow, Baptist, borne & forth broght
    Of a byrde baran, bales to bete.

Gabriel ful godely to thi fader soght,

And seid to þat semely sawes ful swete.

"Þi wyf schal conceyue a child, doute þe nought," 5

Thorgh þe grace of grete God þus he gan hym grete,

"His name schal be calde Ion, take it in thoght;

Many men in his birth with myrthe schul mete."

    With myrthe to mete,

    To the soule sete, 10

      Nedeful to neuen,

    When we awey wende

    Þ[er] we schal long lende,

    He bring vs to heuen.

Blessed be thou, St. John Baptist, born through a miracle!

F. 13.

(2)

Blissed be þou, Baptist, most witty in wone. 15

Was neuer wight in þis worlde more worthi in wede,

Ne neuer body better of blode ne of bone,

But Crist þat for vs his blode wolde blede;

Ne neuer non gretter on ground myght gone,

Ne no man markyd on molde more myghty in mede. 20

Þow art stalworth in stowre & stedfast als stone;

Stande stifly with vs and neghe vs at nede.

    [Þow] neghe vs at nede,

    And make vs at spede

None save Christ was ever greater than thou; be thou our protection!

13. MS. þat.   22. MS. and *crossed out before* at.
                  23. MS. ȝe.

Of God to gete grace.　　　　25
He bring vs to þat blys
Þer myrthes nou mys,
Before his owen face.

(3)

At thy birth, when thy kinsmen came to-gether, thy father wrote that thy name should be John.

Blissed be þow, Baptist; whan þou were borne bare
Of þat buxum body þat þow with-in bredde,　　　　30
When þou were comen to þis world & combrid with care
For sorow and for synne þat men were in stede,
For [gamen] to-gedir þei busked hem ful ȝare,
Ful many [burnes] aboute þe þare þ[ei] w[ere] sprede,
Cosyns kyde of þi kyn, þat wist of þi fare,　　　　35

F. 13 b.

As þe lawe was in land þider were þei lede.
As thei toke to rede
When þei gan hem lede,
Þai fraynd [a] no[m]e
[Þe] child for t[o] calle;　　　　40
He wrote to þem alle,
"His name is callid Ioon."

(4)

When our Lady visited thy mother, she received thee when thou wert born.

Blissed be þou, Baptist, roser of ryght.
When þat me[ns]keful Mary with þi moder mett,
& sche had conceyued Crist þat [maste] is†of myght, 45
Þat swete ful semely here sawes sche sett.
Sche kist here cosyn pertely a-plight,
& thorgh þe grace of here sone ful godely here grett.
Þere sche cawte in clothes þat ilk swete wight,
Þat loutid to Ihesu with-outen any lett.　　　　50
With-outen any leet,
Men said, or thei mett,
[Þo] f[o]des [vn]-borne.
God kepe vs with wyn
And saue vs fro synne　　　　55
Þat we be noght lorne.

---

34. MS. þam was.　　　30. MS. o none.
40. MS. A child forth þei calle.　　　45. MS. þat is ful.
53. MS. oure fadres be borne.

(5)

Blissed be þou, Baptist, I grete þe with good,
Al holy my hert þow hast in þi ho[l]de,
Þow forgoher of Crist þat restid on rood,
Bothe in wele and in wo þou wroght as he wolde.　60
Þat messager þat tolde Mary with ful mylde mode
Þat Goddes Sone wolde be bourn of þat body bolde,
Þ[at] aungel schewed þanne in þat stede þer þei bothe
　　stode,
& broght worde of þat bright, & trewly þanne tolde.
　　　Trewly he tolde　　　　　　　　　　65
　　　To þi fader many folde,
　　　　And neuend [a] no[m]e.
　　For he wolde þe aungel noght leue
　　Ful sore it gan hym greue,
　　　He stode doumbe as ston.　　　　　70

Thou wert Christ's fore-runner; the angel of the Annunci-ation proph-esied to thy father of thy birth.

F. 14.

(6)

Blissed be þou, Baptist, to many folk a frende,
Oure iewel of ioy iugged be lawe,
Faythful in frestyng, oure foos fro vs fende,
Solace to the sory, s[e]kir in thy sawe ;
S[aghtyng] to synful, socour þow sende　　　75
At þe dredeful day whenne † bemes schul blowe,
Þou þat mylde Mary helde in hir h[e]nde
First whan þou were born, as clerkes wele knowe.
　　　As clerkes wele knowe,
　　　Þi fader in a throwe　　　　　　80
　　　　[A poyntil] hade he hent ;
　　Thorgh myracle of þi birthe,
　　In þat tyme of myrth
　　　His speche was hym sent.

Thou, at whose birth Zacharias received his speech, help us at the last day !

(7)

Blissed be thow, Baptist, so ware & so wys.　　85
In wode and in wildirnesse was þi wonyng ;

F. 14 b.

58. MS. honde.　　　　63. MS. þi.
67. MS. on one.　　　　74. MS. sokir.
75. MS. serteyn.　　　　76. MS. whennes.
77. MS. honde.

In the desert
thou didst
refuse soft
raiment and
rich food. Neythir purpil ne palle ne pelle[s] of price,

But of camel skyn þow toke þi clothyng.

Hawes þow [hente] and rotes of þe ryse

Wiᵗʰ borion-and bere in the blomyng,   90

Hony comes [for] ryche mete,—wanted þe þis ;

Folk louely þou lerned vn-to þi lykyng.

> Vn-to þi lykyng,
> Watir drynkyng,
> [Þou] toke it in thoght ;   95
> Sydir ne wyne,
> Were it neueᵣ so fyne,
> Þou neghed it noght.

(8)

When thou
didst baptise
Jesus, the
Holy Ghost
appeared as
a dove. Blissed be þow, Baptist, bothe fer and nere,

Dwellyng in deserte wiᵗʰ ful gode wille ;   100

Þow baptist Ihesu wiᵗʰ-outen any were

In þe flume Iordan, þe faith to fulfille.

F[ro] þe incarnacion † the thre[ttethe] ȝere,

As fel on þe twelft day, he peryd [þe tille] ;

†Þe Holy Gost of heuene he come to þe þere,   105

And as a dowfe on þe he satt þanne ful stille.

> He sat on þe ful stille,
> As it was his wille ;
> A voyce sayde in haast,

F. 15. > " Þis is my child   110
> Bothe meke and mylde,
> In whom me liketh moost."

(9)

Because of
thy rebuke
to Herod,
Herodias
caused her
daughter to
ask for thy
head, and he
granted it. Blissed be þou, Baptist, for thi prechyng,

Þow profet apertely þe poyntes of pees ;

To Herode and Herodias his dere derlyng   115

Resones and right þow rekynde on ryse.

Þou sayd ful scharply in þi saiyng,

And stode stedefastly & thoght not to sese,

89. MS. toke.   91. MS. and.
95. MS. he; t *has been erased after* it.
103. MS. for. of the thred ȝere.   105. MS. vn to þe.

He led hym not lawfully in his likyng
For Philip his brothir wyf þat he to hym chese.   120
  Þe wyf þat he chese,
  Sittyng on deyse,
   Gretly gan hy[r] greue.
  Sche made hir doghter craue
  Þi heued for to haue,   125
  And Herod g[rau]nt hy[r] leue.

(10)

Blissed be þow, Baptist, þi name is ful worthy,
It betokenith Goddes grace as clerkes vs [c]lere,
And o[n] many moo maners men may it discry,
Who so wil lufly listen and [l]ere.   130
Baptist for baptim, so saith þe story,
Of þat worthy wight þat hath no pere ;
Prophet and aungel [þow] may be callyd holy,
And lantern of light þat scyneth ful clere.
  Þow þat schinest so clere,   135
  Goddes darlyng so dere,
   As we in bokes rede,
  Seint Ion þe Baptist,
  Prey for vs to Crist
  Þat heuen be oure mede.   140

Thy name means grace, pray for us that we may win heaven !

F. 15 b.

IV.

[THE SEVEN PENITENTIAL PSALMS]

(1)

[To Goddis worschipe, þat dere us bouȝte,
  To whom we owen to make oure mone
Of alle þe synnes þat we haue wrouȝte
  In ȝouþe, in elde, many oone ;
In þese psalmys þei ben þoruȝ souȝt,   5
  In schame of alle oure goostli foon,
And in to Englische þei ben brouȝt,
  For synne in man to be fordon.]

To the glory of God these Psalms were written agaiunst the Seven Deadly Sins, and are here put into English.

123. MS. hym.   126. MS. gurant hym.
127. Baptist : p *written above.* 129. MS. of.
130. MS. bere.   133. MS. he.
  1-8. *Supplied from* D.

(2)

DOmine, ne in furore tuo arguas me, neque in ira tua
corripias me.

Lord, visit
me not with
Thine anger;
I acknow-
ledge my
sin, and
fear Thy
vengeance.

Lord, in þi angir vptake me noght,
   In thy wreth blame þow not me ;   10
For, if my soule be throgh soght,
   In many a synne my-self I see :
And drede rennith in my thoght
   Þat thow wil a-wreked be ;
But, Lorde, [thow] haast me dere boght,   15
   Spare a while til I be fre.

(3)

Miserere mei, Domine, quoniam infirmus sum ; sana
| me, Domine, quoniam conturbata sunt omnia ossa mea.

Have mercy
on me, for I
am weak ;
save me
when I come
to die !

Mercy, Lord, for I am seke ;
   Heele me, for bresid be my bones ;
My fleesch is freel, my soule [hath] eke
   Ful grete mister to make mones.   20
But, when my cors is cast in creke
   And depe doluen vndir stones,
Ihesu mercyable and meke,
   Lese noght þat thow boghtist ones.

(4)

Et anima mea turbata est ualde; set tu, Domine,
usquequo?

My soul is
grieved ; I
sin against
Thee ever,
and my sole
hope is in
Thy mercy.

And my soule is disturblid sore ;   25
   But, Lord, how longe schal it be so?
If I do synnes more and more,
   Thanne me must suffir peynes moo.
[I] lede a lyfe agayn thy lore
   So wrecchidly þat me is woo ;   30
But thy mercy may me restore,
   Ther is no help whanne it is goo.

15. *So* K.; MS. but.   19. *So* K.
29. *So* K. ; MS. and.

(5)

Conuertere, Domine, et eripe animam meam ; saluum
me fac propter misericordiam [tu]am.

Turne þe, Lord, my soule oute wynne,
    Make me saffe for thy mercy ;
For fowle with fethir ne fysch with fynne   35
Is noon vnstedfaster þanne I.
Whan I thenk what is me with-inne,
    My consciens maketh a careful cry ;
Therfore thy pytee, Lord, vnpynne,
    That I may mende me ther-by.   40

Save thou
my soul, for
no creature
is weaker
than I.

F. 16 b.

(6)

Quoniam non est in morte qui memor sit tui. In
inferno autem quis confitebitur tibi ?

For in deeth is noon þat the thenkith on ;
    Who schal knowlech to the in helle ?
Whan bodyes stynke[n] vnder stone,
    Where soules been no man can telle ;
Therfore, Ihesu, thow felle oure foon,   45
    That al day on vs [y]elpe and [y]helle,
And graunt vs, or we hennes goon,
    Þat we be waschen in mercy welle.

Destroy
Thou our
enemies, and
grant us
mercy ere we
die, for in
death there
is no remem-
brance of
Thee.

(7)

Laboraui in gemitu meo ; lauabo per singulas noctes
lectum meum ; lacrimis meis stratum meum rigabo.

I haue trauaylid in my waylyng ;
    My bedde schal I wasch euery nyght,   50
And with þe terys of my wepyng
    My bedde-straw water, as it is right.
Synne is cause of my mornyng,
    I fele me feynt in goostly [f]ight ;
Therfore I wepe and water wryngge,   55
    As I wele owe and euery wight.

I lament my
sins, as I
well may.

F. 17.

33. MS. meam.   46. MS. þelpe, þhelle.
52. Catch-word synne.   54. So K.; MS. sight.

(8)

Turbatus est a furore oculus meus; inueteraui inter
omnes inimicos meos.

I have
grieved God,
and cry for
mercy.

Myne eghe † for angir disturblid is,
   I eeldid myne enemys amonge ;
Wele I wote I haue doo mys
   And greuyd God with werkes wrong ;   60
And euer when I thenk on this
   I crye on Criste with steuen strong,
And say, "[Lord Ihesu], kyng of blys,
   To thy mercy me vndirfonge ! "

(9)

Discedite a me omnes qui operamini iniquitatem,
quoniam exaudiuit Dominus uocem fletus mei.

Let wrong-
doers depart
from me ; I
betake my-
self to God.

Ye þat doon wrong, gooth fro me alle,   65
   For God my wepyng voys hath herde.
To his fote fayn wil I falle,
   And be chastied with his ȝerde.

F. 17 b.

Now, curteys Kyng, to the I calle,
   Be noght vengeable, put vp thy swerde !   70
In heuen when thow holdist halle,
   Lat me noght be ther-oute sperde !

(10)

Exaudiuit Dominus deprecacionem meam ; Dominus
oracionem meam suscepit.

The Lord has
heard my
prayer, by
the might of
His Passion
may we be
saved !

Oure Lord hath herkenyd my preyer
   And receyuid my oryson ;
Therfore I hope to haue here   75
   Some p[rofi]t of his passion.
He sweet[te] blood and water clere,
   For betyng was his body broune ;
Thow that boghtist man soo dere,
   Lat neuer feend drawe vs [a]doun !   80

57. *So* K. ; MS. eghen.   63. *So* K. ; MS. Ihesu lord.
76. *So* K. ; MS. part.   80. *So* K.

(11)

Erubescant, & conturbentur [vehementer] om*nes* inimici mei; conue*r*tantur, & erubescant ualde uelociter.

Sore a-stonyd and a-schamyd
   Worth alle they þat myn enemys be!
Turnyd and with schame a-tamyd
   Right sone be they, þat I may see!
The world, the feend, the flesch [be] namyd   85
   Ayens man-kynde enemys three;
That I be noght thorgh hem defamyd,
   Derworth Lord, I pray to the. Amen.

May my enemies be dismayed; let not the world, the devil, or the flesh scathe me!

F. 18.

(12)

BEati quoru*m* remisse sunt iniq*ui*tates, & quoru*m*
   tecta sunt peccata.

Blissed be thei whos werkes wrong
   Be forgiuen and synnes hydde,   90
For [thei] þat God hath vndirfong
   In heuen blys ben couth and kydde;
But thei þat ben in lustes long,
   And doon no better than beest or bridde,
Thei may be sekir of stormes strong;   95
   Thoo wrecches are ful woo bytidde.

Blessed be they whose sins are forgiven; but they who live after the flesh have trouble in store.

(13)

Beatus uir cui non imputauit Do*min*us peccatum, nec
est in sp*iri*tu eius dolus.

Blissed be he to whom God re[tt]ith
   No synne, ne hath in goost no gyle;
For at grete prys [the gode Lord] settith
   The man þat meneth neythir wrong ne wyle.   100
Bot he þat conscience vnknittiht
   And yeuith no force it to defyle,
Ayens hym God his wepyn whettith
   To wrekyn hym a litel while.

Blessed be he who does no wrong, but on him who defiles his conscience will God be avenged.

F. 18 b.

91. MS. hem.   97. MS. rekkith; K. rettyt.
      99. MS. god lord it.

(14)

Quoniam tacui, inueterauerunt ossa mea, dum clamarem
tota die.

I cry to Thee,
Lord, for
forgiveness ;
for great is
my need.

I heelde my pees, þerfore my bones   105
   Eldyd while I schuld cry al day ;
I cry, and yit mooste more þanne ones,
   To gete forȝifnes if that I may ;
I haue mister to make mones,
   That haue doon many a wylde outray ;   110
I cry the mercy, Kyng of Thrones,
   I haue trespassed, I say not nay.

(15)

Quoniam die ac nocte grauata est super me manus tua,

Thou hast
afflicted me,
and sin op-
presses me ;
I cry for
mercy.

conuersus sum in erumpna mea, dum configitur spina.

For [b]othe by day and by nyght also
   On me thy honde w[ei]s heuely,
And I am turned i[n] my woo,   115

F. 19.

   Whiles thornes prykke[n] perlously.
Ther prykke[n] me perlously thornes two
   Of synne and pyne, þis fele wele I ;
And therfore, Lord, sithen it is soo,
   I putt me al in thy mercy.   120

(16)

Delictum meum cognitum tibi feci, & iniusticiam meam
non abscondi.

I acknow-
ledge my
sin, and
trust in the
power of
Thy Passion.

My gylt haue I made to þe knowen,
   I haue noght hydde fro the my wrong ;
In shrift shal I be alle a-knowen
   Alle my mysdede, and morne among.
For certys, Lord, we trist and trowen   125
   The welle of grace with stremys strong
Oute of thy faire flessh gan flowen,
   When blood oute of thy hert[e] sprong.

113. MS. lothe.   114. So K. ; MS. was.   115. So K. ; MS. I.
116, 117. MS. prykked ; K. prikketh, prickith.
121. myght crossed out after my.

(17)

Dixi: Confitebor aduersum me in-iusticiam meam
Domino; & tu remisisti impietatem peccati mei.

"To God I schal," I seide, "knowlech
   Agayns my-self my wrong with-inne,"   130
And thow, Lord, as louely lech,
   Forg[a]f the trespas of my synne.
þanne spedith it noght to spare speche,
   To cry on Crist wil I not blynne
That he ne take on me no wreche   135
   For wordes ne werkes þat I begynne.

I said : "I will confess to Christ," and He forgave me.

F. 19 b.

(18)

Pro hac orabit ad te omnis sanctus in tempore oportuno.

Therfore byseke schal euery seynt
   In tyme þat [is þer-to] conable;
For þei be trewe & I am ateynt,
   Thei ben stedfast and I am vnstable.   140
Ther frenschip fonde I neuer feynt;
   Thanne wil I pray, as thei ben able,
That thei wille mouthe my compleynt
   To God þat is so merciable.

I will call upon the saints to be my spokesmen, for they are faithful.

(19)

Verunptamen in diluuio aquarum multarum, ad eum
non approximabunt.

Bot in the floode of waters fele   145
   To hym schal {thei] noght neghe nere,
Them nedith noght þat ben in wele
   The water þat [vs wasches] here;
Bot we that alle day fro hym stele,
   And wrath[en] hym that hath no pere,   150
If he wil vs fro harmes hele,
   Vs nedith to [w]epe water clere.

The saints have no need of tears, but we must weep for our sins.

F. 20.

132. MS. forgyf.   138. *So* K.; MS. þere is so.
146. *So* K.   148. *So* K.; MS. wasches vs.
152. *So* K.; MS. kepe.

(20)

Tu es refugium meum a tribulacione que circumdedit
me ; exultacio mea, erue me a circumd[antibus me].

Thow art my refute in my wo
 That hath envyrounde me aboute ;
[Mi ioye, delyvere me of thoo   155
 That me biclippyn al aboute !]
The feendes fleen to and fro
 To dampne me, this is no dowte ;
But, Lord, when I schal hennys goo,
 Kepe me fro that rewly rowte !   160

(21)

Intellectum tibi dabo, & instruam te in uia hac qua
gradieris ; firmabo super te oculos [meos].

Vndirstondyng I shal the sende,
 And I schal teche the with-alle,
And, in the way that thou schalt wende,
 On the myn eghen festyn I schal.
I am thy God, haue me in mynde,   165
 I made the fre there thow were thralle ;
That no dedely synne the schende,
 Lat witte and wisdom be thi walle.

(22)

Nolite fieri sicut equus & mulus, quibus non est
intellectus.

Ne farith noght as mule or hoors,
 In whiche noon vndirstondyng is ;   170
For so fare thei that ȝyuen no foors
 If they doo neuer soo mykil mys.
Thenk that thy coruptible coors
 Is noght but wormes mete i-wys ;
Therfore in myrth haue thow remoors,   175
 And euer among thenk wele on this.

(23)

In chamo & freno maxillas eorum constringe, qui non
approximant ad te.

In bernacle or bridell thow constreyne
  [The] chekes of hem þat neghes þe noght!
For certys, Lord, bot thow refreyne,
  We schul do synne in euery thoght.   180
The world is noght but synne and peyne
  And wrecchednesse þat men han wroght;
Of this meschief I me compleyne
  To Ihesu that hath me dere boght.

If thou constrain us not, we sin continually.

F. 21

(24)

Multa flagella peccatoris; sperantem autem in Domino
misericordia circumdabit.

Manyon is þe sadde betyng   185
  That to the synful schal be-tyde,
Bot he that is in God trostyng
  Shal mercy kepe on euery syde;
Whan wrecches schul ther hondes wryng,
  That were so ful of pompe and pryde,   190
Than schul the sauyd soules synge
  For blys that they schul in abyde.

Those that trust in God shall be saved, but sinners shall suffer sorely.

(25)

Letamini in Domino, & exultate, iusti; & gloriamini,
omnes recti corde.

In oure Lord be mery and gladde,
  Ȝe that of ryghtful hert[e] be,
For he þat was on the rode spradde   195
  Now sitteth in his fadres see.
In sight of hym schul we be [c]ladde
  As aungels that bee † bright [of] blee;
Ihesu, graunt vs to be ladde †
  So that we may that sight[e] see!   Amen.   200

Rejoice we in our ascended Lord, and pray that we may come to Him!

F. 21 b.

178. *So* K.; MS. of.   197. MS. gladde.
198. MS. in bright; K. brith of.   199. *So* K.; MS. gladde.

(26)

DOmine, ne in furore tuo arguas me, ne*que* in ira
　　tua corripias me.

Lord, blame me noght whan thow art wrot*h*e,
　　Vptake me noght in thy hastynesse,
If I haue lyued as the is loth*e*,
　　Vnkynde aȝeins thy kyndenesse.
For wanton worde and ydel othe　　　　　　　205
　　And many a werk of wyckednesse,
I drede thy dome aȝeins me goth
　　Bot grace go † with rightfulnesse.

(27)

*Quoniа*m sagitte tue infixe sunt michi, et confirmasti
sup*er* me manu*m* tuam.

For thin arowes ben in me pight,
　　Thow hast seet fast on me thin honde;　　　210
And, as man with-oute myght,
　　I wexe weyk as is the wonde.
Bot, Lord, meyntyn thow thi right,

　　Supporte thi man that may not stonde,
And comfort thow thi febil knyght　　　　　　215
　　That fer is flemyd oute of thy lond.

(28)

Non est sanitas in carne mea, a facie ire tue; non est
pax ossib*us* meis, a fa[cie peccatorum meorum].

For in my flesch*e* ther is no hele
　　In p*r*esence of thi w[re]th[l]i face,
To my bones is pees ne wele
　　For synnes that me thus deface.　　　　　　220
Therfore, when deth schal wit*h* me dele,
　　I se no help, Lorde, bot thi grace;
My wyld[e] will, my wittes frele
　　Eencombre me when I trespace.

208. *So* K.; MS. goth.
218. MS. worthi.

(29)

Quoniam iniquitates mee super*gresse* sunt caput meum,
sicut onus [graue] grauate [sunt super me].

For now aboue my heued ere growen   225
    The werkes of my wykkednesse,
And vp-on me synnes be throwen
    As birdeyn of grete heuynesse.
I may me no[whe]r now bestowen
    To hyde me fro thy hastynesse ;   230
Neuertheles ȝit, as we trowen,
    Thi mercy passeth rightwisnesse.

My sins oppress me ; I fear Thy wrath, but trust to Thy mercy.

F. 22 b.

(30)

Putruerunt & corrupte sunt cica*tri*ces mee, a facie
insipiencie † mee.

Now be my woundes roten and rank
    Before the face of my foly,
And, sithen I [fir]st in synne sank,   235
    Can I noght bot mercy cry.
Now, Crist þat reysed hym þat stank,
    The brothir of Marthe and [of] Mary,
So bryng me fro this brery bank
    To heuen blys aboue the sky.   240

My sin is as a sore disease ; Lord, who didst raise Lazarus from corruption, bring me to Heaven !

(31)

Miser factus sum & curuatus su*m* usq*ue* in fine*m* ; tota
die contristatus ingrediebar.

I wexe a wrecche in-to the last ende,
    Croked and careful yede al day ;
Myrth may noon come in my mynde
    When I thenk on my longe way.
I wote wele I mote hennys wende,   245
    Bot whedir and when I can not say ;
Therfore my boxom bakke I bende
    That Crist me kepe, for he best may.

The thought of death oppresses me, but I pray to Christ.

F. 23.

229. *So* K.; MS. nothir.   233. MS. insipiciencie.
235. MS. last.   238. *So* K.

(32)

Quoni*am* lumbi mei impleti sunt illusionib*us*, & non
est sanitas in carne mea.

For ful of fayry be my reynes,
   And in [my] flesch ther is noon helth ;   250
Therfore of g*r*ace sende me greynes,
   That I may fle all fleschly felth.
Let neuer the feende w*ith* [al] his traynes
   Stert vpon me w*ith* hi̇s stelth*e*,
To sett on me his firy ch[e]ynes,   255
   For weldyng of this worldes welth*e*.

(33)

Afflictus sum, & humiliatus nimis ; rugiebam a gemitu
cordis mei.

I was torment and made ful meke,
   I rorid for waylyng of my hert ;
Oure foorme fadres a [for]warde breke ;
   Therfore alle we be woo-bygert ;   260
And I ther-to my synnes eke ;

   What wonder if my hert[e] smert ?
Therfore thy mercy, Lord, I seke,
   For I may noght thy hand astert.

(34)

Domine, ante te omne desid*erium* meum, & gemitus
meus a te non [est] absconditus.

Lorde, alle my desire is the byforne,   265
   My sorow is noght fro the hydde ;
For, if my soule schuld be forlorne,
   What were I better than beest or brydde ?
Therfore, Ih*e*su, of Iewis boorne,
   God and man in erthe kydde,   270
Lat neuer that tresoure be to-toorne,
   That thow were fore soo sore betydde.

(35)

Cor meum conturbatum est in me ; dereliquit me uirtus
mea ; & lumen oculorum meorum, & ipsum [non est
mecum].

My hert in me disturblyd is,
   My vertu hath forsaken me,
Myn eghen sight with me now nys,   275
   My Saueour may I noght see ;
I erre al day and do amys,
   I stomble as thei that blynde be,
And synne ywys is cause of this ;
   Mercy, Ihesu, for thy pitee !   280

I am in sore trouble and perplexity through my sin ; have mercy on me, Lord !

F. 24.

(36)

Amici mei & proximi mei aduersum me appropin-
quauerunt & steterunt.

My neighbors and thei that frendes were
   Neyghden and a-ȝeinst me stode ;
In welth a man may wysdom lere,
   Bot wele were hym that vnderstode.
[N]ow frendes flokken euery-where,   285
   As fowlys doon aftir ther fode ;
Bot, be a man dede and broght on bere,
   Many be feynt and fewe be gode.

In our prosperity our friends are many, but few remember us when we die.

(37)

[Et qui iuxta me erant, de longe steterunt ; et vim
faciebant qui querebant animam meam.

Thei stode afer that where me nygh,
   Thei strenghed hem that my sowle sought,   290
The world was fals, the fend was slygh,
   The flesch dide so that me forthought.
Therfor to Godde than y fleygh
   With lowly herte, and him besought
To yeve confort fro hevene an heegh   295
   Of werkis that i hadde myswrought.]

Temptations assailed me, and I fled to God for comfort.

275. MS. is *crossed out before* nys.
285. MS. how.   289-96. *So* K.

(38)

Et qui inquirebant mala *michi*, locuti sunt uanitates,
& dolos tota die med[itabantur].

My enemies
laboured
against me,
but when
they are
dead, the
truth will be
manifest.

F. 21 b.

And thei that thoght to do me skathe
Spekyn wordes al in vayn,
And alle the day, bothe late and rathe,
Thei thoght on gyle and vpon trayn.   300
Bot when thei fede moght and mathe,
And breres growen aboue her brayn,
Thanne schal the sothe hym-self vnswathe,
How synne hath many a soule slayn.

(39)

Ego autem, tanq*uam* surdus, non audieba*m* ; & sicut
mutus non ap*er*iens os suum.

I was as one
who is deaf
and dumb,
but Christ
will punish
sinners.

Bot I as deef man no-[þing] herde,   305
And, as doumbe that [no mouth vndoth],
So sp[a]ryd I, and speche sperde ;
Bot whan I spake I seyde soth ;
For [he] that Iewes so foule with ferde,
That wote how eu*er*y gyl[e] goth,   310
Ful sore wil smyte w*ith* his ȝerde,
Bot men [a]mende hem þ*at* mys-doth.

(40)

Et f*a*ctus sum sicut homo non audiens, & no*n* habens
in ore suo [redarguciones].

I was as one
who is deaf
and dumb ;
but, Lord,
grant that
we may
repent !

F. 25.

I be-cam as man [that] myght noght here,
Ne hadde in mouth noon opynnyng ;
I saugh the synful gladde of chere,   315
And went[e] forth ful sore syghyng.
Bot, Lord, þ*at* boghtest man so dere,
Let hym no blys in balys bryng,
But sende hym myght to amende hy*m* here,
And gr*a*unt hym gr*a*ce of vprysyng.   320

300. on *added above the line.*
301. MS. moght and *written over* mothe and *crossed out.*
305. MS. noght.   306. MS. vndoth no mouth.
307. *So* K. ; MS. speryd.   309. *So* K.
310. *So* K. ; MS. gylt.   312. *So* K.   313. *So* K.

(41)

Quoniam in te, Do*m*ine, speraui, tu exaudies me,
Domine Deus meus.

Lorde, for I haue trest in the,
  My Lord, my God, thow schalt me here,
For reuerence of that Lady fre
  That ȝaf the soke and hath no pere.
To that Lady betake I me,   325
  That woneth aboue the clowdes clere ;
For, while sche sitte[th] neghc th[i] see,
  I hope to spede of my preyer.

Lord, hear me, for the sake of Thy Mother !

(42)

Quia dixi : Nequando super*g*aud[e]ant michi inimici
mei ; et du*m* commouentur pedes [mei, super me magna
locuti sunt].

For I haue seyd, " Lord mercyable,
  Let noght [vp me] my foos be gladde ! "   330
For, while I stere my feet vnstable,
  Vpon me thei grete wordes made.
Bot Crist, that art so comfortable,
  Make her floures falle and fade,
And the to plese make me able :   335
  In synne wil I no more waade.

Let not my enemies flourish, but keep me in Thy grace !

F. 25 b.

(43)

Quoniam ego in flagella paratus sum, & dolor meus in
conspectu meo semper.

For I am redy to be betyn,
  My sorow is euer in my sight,
To do [h]is wille wil I gode letyn,
  Aȝeins my God wil I noght fight.   340
Now, Lord, þat woldest blode [out] sweten
  For hem þat to deeth were dight,
So sende me grace for to gretyn
  Water þat may my hert[e] light !

I will obey God's will ; Lord, grant me to weep for sin !

327. *So* K. ; MS. sitte, the.   329. MS. super*g*audiant.
         330. *So* K. ; MS. vpon.

(44)

Quoniam iniquitatem meam annunciabo, & cogitabo
pro *peccato* meo.

For I my wrong schal tellén oute,   345

F. 26.
And for my synne thenk I schal

Pride, lech-
ery, envy
and wrath
imperil the
soul at
death.
How it is perilous to be prow[t]e,

And lecherie may lesyn alle.

Enuye and wrath of hert[e] stoute

Shal stand a man in litel stalle,   350

When he is clothed in a clowte,

To wonne [with]-in a wormys walle.

(45)

Inimici autem mei uiuu*nt*, & confirmati sunt supe*r*
me; & multiplicati sunt qui [oderunt me inique].

My enemies
are strong,
but I will
pray to
Christ,
whom Judas
sold, to save
me.
But myn enemyes ben quyk and bolde,

And strenghed on me myghtily;

Thei be encresyd many folde   355

That haue me hatyd wrongfully;

But Goddys Lombe, *þat* Iudas solde

For thritty pens vnrightfully,

[I] will pray to be in his folde,

To do his byddyng boxomly.   360

(46)

Qui retribuu*nt* mala pro bonis detrahebant michi, qui
sequeba[r] bonitate*m*.

F. 26 b.
Thei *þat* for good euel quyten,

The wicked
backbited
me, but God
will punish
them.
For I good folowed, bakbytid me;

Bot thei *þat* thus falsly bakbyten,

Ful dredeful may ther hertes be;

For God schal alle ther wordes writen,   365

And schewe, *þat* alle the world schal see,

How scharply he schal [al] them smyten,

That wolde noght that vice fle.

345. MS. ego cognosco *crossed out after* meam.
347. MS. prowde.   352. *So* K.
359. *So* K.   361. MS. sequebat.
367. *So* K.

(47)

Ne derelinquas me, Domine Deus meus ; ne discesseris
a me.

My Lord, my God, forsake me noght,
   Depart thow me neuer the fro,   370
Hold vp thi hous þat thow hast wroght,
   Forsake noght, Lord, my soule so !
This is thi woorde, thow hast it boght ;
   Elynges it were if thow were goo ;
Therfore, Ihesu, lett neuer thoght   375
   Ne worde ne dede part vs a-two.

*Lord, for-
sake not my
soul ; Thou
hast redeem-
ed this
world, let me
not be
parted from
Thee !*

(48)

Intende in adiutorium meum, Domine, Deus salutis
mee.

To my helpyng take thow hede,
   My Lord, my God, and al my helth !
Be neghe me, Lord, whan I haue nede,
   And wysse me whan I am in welth.   380
With gostely food[e] thow me fede,
   And kepe me from al flesshly felth,
And graunt me grace for some gode dede
   To se the fruyt of goostly telth.

F. 27.

*Do Thou,
Lord, guide
me, feed me,
keep me
from sin,
and grant
me to per
severe !*

(49)

Miserere mei, Deus, secundum magnam misericordiam
tuam.

Mercy, God, of my mysdede,   385
   For thi mercy that mykil is ;
Let thi pite spryng and sprede,
   Of thi mercy that I noght mys.
After goostly grace I grede ;
   Gode God, thow graunt me this,   390
That I mote here my lyfe lede
   So that I doo no more amys.

*Lord, have
mercy upon
me, and
keep me
from sin!*

(50)

Et *secundum* multitudine*m* misera*c*ionu*m* tuaru*m*, dele
iniquitatem meam.

And, aftir thi me*r*cyes þat ben fele,
 Lord, for-do my wykkednesse ;

Help [me] for to hyde and hele   395
 The blames of my bre[c]helnes.
Ʒif any strengh[e] wil me stele
 Out of the close of thi clennes,
Wys me, Lorde, in wo and wele,
 And kepe me for thi kyndenes.   400

(51)

Amplius laua me ab iniquitate mea, & a pecc*a*to me
munda me.

More-ou*er*e wassche me of my synne,
 And fro my gyltes clense me ;
Enserche my soule bothe oute & ynne,
 That it no more defoulyd bee ;
And, as thyn hert[e] cleef a-twynne   405
 With doolful deth on the rode tre,
So let me neuer werke begynne
 Lorde, bot if it lyke the.

(52)

Q*uoni*am iniquitatem mea*m* ego cognosco, | & pecc*a*tu*m*
meu*m* contra me est semp*er*.

For alle my wykkednes I knowe,
 And my synne is eu*er* my sight agayne ; 410
And therfore let thi pite growe,
 Ihe*s*u, þat were of Iewis slayne ;
For ryche and po*r*e, hygh and lowe,
 And euer[y] wight, I am certayne,
On domesday, whan thow schal blowe, 415
 Of thi mercy wil† be fayne.

(53)

Tibi soli peccaui, malum coram te feci ; ut iustificeris
in sermonib*us* [tuis, et vincas cum iudicaris].

To the onely trespassyd haue I,
    Wroght wikkedly and the not qwemed ;
Þo werkys askys rightfully
    Thow hast þe victory when þou art demed.   420
Demyd thow were wrongfully
    For me þat haue [thi] f[eit]h for[y]emed ;
Bot, Lord, let me neuer doo why
    That I be fro thi face flemed.

I have sinned against Thee, Who wert unjustly condemned for my sin, let me not be banished from Thee !

(54)

Ecce enim in iniquitatib*us* conceptus su*m*, & in
peccat*is* concepit me mater mea.   F. 28 b.

Byholde, in synne I was conceyued   425
    Of my moder, as men ere [a]lle ;
Of my fadir noght I receyued
    Bot boon and flesch freel to falle ;
Bot sithen thi flesch, Lorde, was p*er*ceyued,
    Where it was leyd ful streyt in stall,   430
Was ther noon synful man deceyued,
    That wolde on[to] thi mercy calle.

Lo, I was born in sin, but through Thy Incarnation all may be saved.

(55)

Ecce enim ueritatem dilexisti† ; inc*er*ta &† occulta
sap*ienc*ie tue manifestasti m*ich*i.

Byholde, thow hast louyd the right,
    And schewed me conseil of thi witte,
How thorow m*er*cy and thorow myght   435
    Two kyndes been to-gedir knytte :
[Thral is fre and knave is knyght],
    God is man, as gospel writte,
And, if my soule in p*er*ell is pyght,
    Mercy, God, and help thow itt !   440

Thou hast made known to me how God is become man ; help Thou my soul !

422. *So* K. ; MS. my flesch forþemed.
426. *So* K ; MS. telle.   432. MŞ. on ; K. to.
433. MS. dilexixisti ; & in occulta.   437. *So* K.

(56)

F. 29.

Asperges me, Domine, ysopo, & mundabor; lauabis
me, & super niuem dealbabor.

If I sin,
grant me re-
pentance,
for Thou art
dearer than
worldly joy.

With holy water thow schalt me spryng,
  And as the snowe I schal be quyte;
For, if my soule in synne synk,
  With wepying water it may be qwyte.
Deedly draghtes if I drynk,   445
  Of repentaunce gyf me respyte;
For, on the trestly who-so thynk,
  In worldes welth is no delyte.

(57)

Auditui meo dabis gaudium & leticiam, & exultabunt
ossa humiliata.

Direct me
and give me
joy, let me
not die un-
forgiven!

To my herying thow schal yeue
  Gladnes, to glade my boones meke;   450
In lowenes lerne me to leue;
  Be noght to fer when I the seke;
And let me noght to deeth be dreue,
  Derworth Lorde, I the beseke,
Til my synnes be foryeue   455
F. 29 b. Of thoght and worde and dede[s] eke.

(58)

Auerte faciem tuam a peccatis meis, & omnes
iniquitates meas dele.

Look not on
my sins; I
trust in Thy
mercy, and
repent.

Fro my synnes turne thi face,
  Put al my wykkednes awey;
Greet is my gilt, gretter thi grace,
  And elles fayleth oure f[ey].   460
Defautes many þat me deface
  Makes me syng welaway
And crye mercy when I trespasse;
  I woot ther is noon othir [wey].

456. So K.   460. So K.; MS. faith.
        464. So K.; MS. grace.

(59)

Cor mundum crea in me, Deus, & spiritum rectum
innoua in uisceribus meis.

God, make my hert[e] clene,	465
A rightful goost in me renewe,	
Fro seuen synnes make me schene,	
Where-so thow goo þat I may sewe.	
Allas! thi t[our]ment and thi tene	
Made thi brest and bak al blewe;	470
Now g[rau]nt[e], Crist, it may be sene	
With-innet my hert, thy hydouse hewe!	

Cleanse me from my sin, and let Thy Passion be seen in me!

F. 30.

(60)

Ne proicias me a faci[e] tua, & spiritum sanctum tuum
ne auferas a me.

Cast me noght fro thi visage;	
Take noght awey thi holy goost;	
For in the sight of that ymage	475
Is fulsomnesse and myrth[e] moost.	
I haue ben wylde & doon outrage,	
Vnwisely wroght, as thow wele woost;	
Therfore sende me some corage	
To fight agaynes the fendes oost.	480

Cast me not away from Thy sight, though I have sinned against Thee.

(61)

Redde michi leticiam salutaris tui, et spiritu principali
confirma me.

Of thyn hele зelde me blisse,	
And strenght me with thi spirit cheef;	
Alle my fyue wittes thow wysse,	
That I may lyf as the is leef;	
And, as thow may my langour lysse,	485
That broghtest man to grete bonchef,	
So lat me neuer mercy mysse	
When I am greuyd with goostly greef.	

Strengthen and direct me, grant me Thy mercy!

F. 30 b.

469. MS. turoment.   471. MS. gurant.
472. *So* K.; MS. with inne with my.   473. MS. facias.
477. outrage *written twice and crossed out the first time.*
483. me *crossed out after* alle.   485. аs *inserted above the line.*

(62)

Docebo iniquos uias tuas ; & impij ad te conuertentur.

I will teach
the sinful
what shame
Thou hast
suffered for
them.

The wycked I schal th[i] weyes teche ;
   Th[e] synful schal to the conuert ;   490
Synful man, beware of wreche,
   And thenk on Crist with al thin hert,
How he become thi louely leche,
   And for thi sake ful sore smert ;
Ther was no scorne ne spytouse speche,   495
   Dispite ne strook þat hym astert.

(63)

Libera me de sanguinibus, Deus, Deus salutis [mee, et
exultabit lingua mea iusticiam tuam].

Deliver me
from bloodguiltiness,
Thou that
didst shed
Thy blood
for us.

F. 31.

Delyuer me fro blameful bloode,
   Almyghty God of alle my helth ;
Than schal my tonge be myry of moode
   To telle[n] of thi ryghtful telth.   500
Thi ryghtful bloode ran doun on rode,
   That wasshe vs fro oure flesshly felth,
And many a storme agayne [thow] stoode,
   To wys vs fro the worldes welth.

(64)

Domine, labia mea aperies ; & os meum annun[ciabit
laudem tuam].

Grent is Thy
glory, Who
dost absolve
us from
deadly sin.

My lyppes, Lorde, thow schal vndoo,   505
   And my mouthe schal thi preysyng spelle ;
Thi mercy and þi myght alsoo
   Parfitely can no man telle ;
For, whanne we dedely synnes doo,
   Thei vs demen to goo to helle ;   510
Bot, whanne we sees & can sey 'hoo ! ',
   Thi mercy is oure wasshyng welle.

489. So K. ; MS. the.   503. MS. vs ; K. the.
507. þi inserted above the line.

(65)

Quoniam si voluisses sacrificium, dedissem utique;
[holocaustis non delectaberis].

For, yif thow woldist haue had offryng,
    I had it ȝeuen with hert[e] fre ;
Bot thow schal haue† noon lykyng   515
    In sacrifyce of that degree ;
For thow were offrid vp hongyng
    For mannes sake on rode tree,
And of thin hert gan bloode oute sprynge,
    Wherfore my hert I offre the.   520

Thou gavest Thy Heart for man, I give my heart to Thee.

F. 31 b.

(66)

Sacrificium Deo spiritus contribulatus ; cor c[ontritum
et humiliatum, Deus, non despicies].

To God it is a sacrifyce,
    The goost þat is [a]greuyd sore ;
Meke hert schal thow noght despice,
    Whiles repentaunce may it restore.
I haue forslowthid, Lorde, thi seruice,   525
    And litel leuyd aftir thi lore,
Bot now I repent and aryse ;
    Mercy, Ihesu, I wil no more.

I have not served Thee aright; but Thou desirest repentance, and I will return to Thee.

(67)

Benigne fac, Domine, in bona uoluntate tua [Sion, ut
edificentur muri Ierusalem].

With benigne wil do to Syon
    Þat Ierusalem walles were vp wroght ;   530
Ierusalem, as saith seint Ion,
    Is Holy Chirche, þat errith noght.
Too testamentes cordyng in oon,
    Thise were walles to-gedir broght,
When Crist hym-self was corner stoon,   535
    That mannes soule had dere boght.

Thou art the Corner-Stone of Holy Church, whose walls are the two Testaments.

F. 32.

515. MS. haue a noon; K. have no.
521. MS. is *crossed out after* God.

(68)

Tunc acceptabis sacrificium iusticie, [oblaciones et
holocausta ; tunc imponent super altarem tuum
vitulos].

Thanne shalt thow sacrifyce accepte
    Of ryghtwysnesse and treuthe entier,
And calueren aftir thy precepte
    Sall men leyn on thine autier.   540
On Caluarie a calf there crepte,
    Crist on crosse both clene and clere ;
For teris that his modir wepte,
    He schild vs fro the fendes fere ! Amen.

(69)

D Omine, exaudi oracionem, & cla[mor meus ad te
    uehiat].

Lord, thow herken my preyer,   545
    And to the lat come my cry ;
Wouchesauf to lysten and here
    The moon that I make mekely.
To cry on the with careful chere
    There [nedith] noon † so mykil as I ;   550
Therfore my steuen strenght and stere,
    That I noght speke vnspedely.

(70)

Non auertas faciem tuam a me ; in quacunque [die
tribulor, inclina ad me aurem tuam].

Turne noght, Lord, fro me thi face,
    Bowe doun thin ere when me is wo,
Lat growe greynes of thi grace   555
    That quencheth synnes and peynes also ;
In wey of charite thow me chace,
    [Thi] feyth lat me noght falle fro,
And help me þat I noght trespace
    Vp hope of mercy neuer moo.   560

544. fed *erased after* fendes. Amen *written in a less formal hand.*
550. MS. there noon doth ; K. that nedith no man.
558. *So* K.; MS. in.   trespace *crossed out after* noght.

(71)

In quacunq*ue* die innocauer*o* te, uelociter [exaudi me].

<table>
<tr><td>

Euery day when I the calle,
   Redely thow listen me,
For ryghtful ere thi werkes alle,
   Bot mercy is thy propyrte ;
Therfore if I frely falle
   In-to synnes that I schuld fle,
Putt me noght oute of thy halle,
   But help me turne agayn to the.

</td><td>565</td><td>

Have mercy
on me when
I fall !

</td></tr>
</table>

(72)

Quia defecerunt sicut fumus die[s] mei, [et ossa mea sicut cremium aruerunt].

<table>
<tr><td>

For my lijf-dayes are liyk smoke
   That faylide and a-weyward hy3ede ;
My boones [ben] dryede and forsoke,
   Ry3t as a þing þat is forfryede :
Of Crist may wele þese wordis be spoke,
   That on the crois was doon and driede ;
Whanne his blysful brest was broke,
   For drouthe and þriste lowde he cryede.

</td><td>570

575</td><td>

F. 83.
" My life
pines away,
my bones are
dried up : "
these words
prefigure
Christ.

</td></tr>
</table>

(73)

Percussus sum ut fenum, & aruit cor meu*m*, q*ui*a oblitus sum comedere panem meu*m*.

<table>
<tr><td>

Smyten I was lijk gras or hay,
   Myn herte waxide drye and deed,
For I forgate what maner of way
   That I schulde ete myn owne breed.
To peyne me was al þeir play,
   They þraste þornes þoru myn heed,
Dispitously þanne spedden they
   With blood to make my body reed.

</td><td>580</td><td>

" I was
afflicted and
persecuted,
crowned
with thorns
and
scourged."

</td></tr>
</table>

569. MS. diei. *Catch-words* For my. *Here the handwriting changes.*
571. K. beth drie.

(74)

A uoce gemitus mei adhesit os | meum carni mee.

"My
kinsfolk
lamented
Me, I was
scorned by a
thief, and
given gall
and
vinegar."

For the voys of my weylyng   585
   Vn-to my fleisch my boones can schrynke ;
[Y say my cosyn Jon mornynge],
   I say my modir in swownynge synk ;
I herde a theef me scoornynge ;
   Galle and eisel was my drynk ;   590
I wepte as a child of ȝeris ȝing,
   On þis myscheef whenne I can þink.

(75)

Similis factus sum pellicano solitudinis ; factus sum
sicut nicticorax in domicilio.

"Like the
pelican I
gave Myself
to death ;
like the
night-crow I
saw through
the darkness
of man's sin
My plan of
salvation."

I was maad liyk the pellycan,
   That vpon wylde[r]nesse hym-silf sleeþ,
So redily to the roode I ran,   595
   For mannys soule to suffre deeþ ;
And, as þe nyȝt-crowe in hir hous can
   By nyȝt[e] se to holte and heeþ,
So purposide I to saue man,
   For hym I ȝaf my goost and breeþ.   600

(76)

Vigilaui, et factus sum sicut pas|ser solitarius in tecto.

"I was cut
off from
mankind,
My flesh was
torn."

I wook, and was maad lijk a sparowe
   That in þe roof restiþ † solitarye ;
Vpon þe tre my neest was narowe,
   There-on myȝte I no briddis carye.
As erþe is hurlyd vndir harowe,   605
   So was þe fleisch þat sprang of Marye ;
In þis world [is] noon so scharp arowe
   As was þe turment that [me gan tarie].

587. *So* K.   594. *So* K.
602. MS. restiþ so solitarye.   607. *So* K.
608. *So* K. ; MS. hadde Ie.

(77)

Tota die exprobrabant † michi inimici mei, et qui
laudabant me aduersum me iurabant.

For al the day they [hadde] me [in] scoorne,
    Men that myn enemyes were,   610
And þo that preysiden me biforne
    Aftirward aȝeyns me swere.
Thanne was I to-tuggid and to-torne,
    Foot and hond, iȝen and eere,
To ech a lyme lijf [hadde] lorne ;   615
    Myn heed þei corownyd wiþ þorn of brere.

*" My
enemies
scorned Me,
My friends
turned
against Me ;
I endured
My Pas-
sion."*

[78]

Quia cinerem tanquam panem manducabam, et potum   F. 34 b.
meum cum fletu miscebam.

For askis as it were breed I ete,
    Wiþ wepyng I mengide my drink among,
For loue of man me þouȝte it swete
    To suffre scoorn and sorowe strong ;   620
For, siþen Adam the lawe lete
    Thoru hir þat of his rib[be] sprong,
Was neuere man to mercy meete
    Til I hadde suffrid wo and wrong.

*" I suffered
for love of
man ; I alone
could atone
for Adam's
sin."*

(79)

A facie ire [et] indignacionis tue, quia eleuans allisisti
me.

A-fer fro þe face of þi greuaunce   625
    Thow droue me down wiþ vprisyng,
Fadir, I was to thi plesaunce
    Lyfte up as God in God dwellyng ;
But, for to stynte al disturbaunce
    Of man þat synnede not ceessyng,   630
Thow droue me adoun to chese a chaunce,
    As man for man the deeþ takyng.

*" I was lifted
up before
Thee, Father,
and cast
down for
man's sake.*

F. 35

609. MS. exprobrabrant ; [hadde] me [in], so K.
615. So K. ; MS. and.

(80)

Dies mei sicut vmbra declinauerunt, & ego sicut
fenum arui.

"My
strength
ebbed away;
the cen-
turion
hailed me
as God's
Son."

My dayes passiden as schadow of liȝt,
  And I wexide drye as dooþ the gras;
I wente as man with-outen myȝt,   635
  Where-so I trad was blody tras.
Whanne I þus deolfully was diȝt,
  That neuere dyde ony trespas,
Centurio seyde, "We doon vnriȝt,
  For truly Goddis Sone this was."   640

(81)

Tu autem, Domine, in eternum permanes, & memoriale
tuum in generacionem et generacionem.

Thou art
God for ever,
as Man Thou
wert slain
by men.

For ceertis, Lord, þou dwellist euere,
  Thy mynde abidiþ in euery kynde;
For thi Godheed was noyed neuere,
  There was no þing þat þee myȝte scheende.
Th[i] manheed myȝte men wel disseuere,   645
  Therof þei made a ruful eende,

F. 35 b.

Therfore ech man is þee the leuere,
  That þis mater haþ wel in mynde.

(82)

Tu exurgens, Domine, misereberis Syon, quia tempus
miserendi eius, quia venit tempus.

Have merc
on Holy
Church!

Thow schalt vprise & Syon ruwe,
  For tyme is come of hir mercy;   650
Syon is Holy Chirche trewe
  Of men þat lyuen Cristenly.
A stidefast seed in hir þou sewe,
  And tauȝtist hir so tendirly
How þat sche schulde synne eschewe   655
  And loue thee moost hertily.

641. permanes; s *added above the line.*
645. *So* K.; MS. the.

(83)

Quoniam placuerunt seruis tuis lapides eius, & terre
eius miserebu*ntur*.

For þi seruau*n*tis [hir] stoonys lykide,
 And on hir þei schulen haue pyte ;
Crist, corner stoon, x*ij* stoones pykide,
 [His] x*ij* apostlys for to be.   660
They haue hem-silf a dongeou*n* dikide
 In Syon, as men may se,
That whoso † be w*ith* synne entrikide
 May sauely to þat strengþe fle.

She is built
on the
foundation-
stones of the
Twelve
Apostles.

F. 36.

(84)

Et timebunt gentes nomen tuum, Do*m*ine, & om*n*es
[reges] terre glo*r*iam tua*m*.

[And folkus schul thi name drede,   665
 Alle erthely kynges doute thi blisse,
That privest princes of here pryde,
 That wantounly here wittes wisse.
Right as the lust thu maist men lede,
 Save and sle and langour lisse,   670
But wo is hym that doth that dede
 Wherfor he mot thi mercy mysse.

All nations
shall praise
Thee who
rulest all.
men.

(85)

Quia edificavit Dominus Syon, et videbitur in gloria
sua.

For God hath housed Syon,
 And yn his blisse hit schal be sowen
Wan holi chirche be maad on   675
 Yn hevene as we triste and trowen ;
And we schulle to gladnesse goon,
 That in grace on grounde now growen ;
Graunte God that y be on
 That be noght out of hevene throwen !   680

May I be
among those
that rejoice
with Thy
Church in
Heaven !

657. *So* K.
663. *So* K.; MS. whoso not be.

660. *So* K. ; MS. and.
665-80. *So* K.

(86)

Respexit in oracionem humilium, et non sprevit precem eorum.]

God hears
the humble,
but loves
not the
proud.

The orisoun of þe meke he siȝ,
 And not dispiside her preyer ;
But hem þat are of herte hiȝ
 Ne be not to him so leef and dere
As tho þat alle vices fliȝ.   685
Of Ihesu Crist a man may lere,
For he to noon estaat ne stiȝ,
 But euere was low in word & chere.

(87)

Scribantur hec in generacione altera, populus qui creabitur laudabit Dominum.

For our sins
was Christ
so sorely
afflicted.

F. 36 b.

In anoþer kynrede lete þese be writen,
 Thanne schal preise God þe peple vnbore, 690
For who-so may þese wondris wyten
 Ouȝte to þanke God þerfore ;
And þat is for we falsly flyten,
 Hys fair[e] flesch was al to-tore ;
For mannys sake so sore smyten 695
 Was neuere noon siþen ne bifore.

(88)

Quia prospexit de excelso sancto suo ; Dominus de celo in terram aspexit.

He saw from
Heaven how
man was
oppressed
by Satan.

For he say fro his holy heiȝt,
 To erþe oure Lord say out of heuene,
He say man walke vndir þe weiȝt
 Of alle þe deedly synnes seuene ; 700
He say man þoru þe feendis sleiȝt
 Lygge slepynge in [a] synful sweuene ;
Therfore he vouchide saaf to fiȝt
 To God and man were oonyd euene.

(89)

Ut audiret gemitus compeditorum, ut solueret filios interemptorum.

To heere the weilynge and þe wo   705   To redeem
   Of hem that were in care bounde,   man He be-
And to vnbynde the kynde of þo   came Man.
   That were killid wiþ deedly wounde,   F. 37.
For þese causis and for mo
   Was God maad man to go on grounde;   710
Therfore men schulden not falle him fro,
   For he suffride for hem many a stounde.

(90)

Ut annuncient in Syon nomen Domini, & laudem eius in Iherusalem.

For they schulden in Syon teche   He has
   Oure Lordis name þat holy is,   taught the
And in Ierusalem hys preisyng preche,   715   Church to
   Hym-silf he cam and tauȝte þis.   praise Him;
þere may no wiȝt wiþstonde his wreche,   Almighty.
   There is no nay þere he seith ȝhis;
Therfore preise we hym wiþ speche,
   And drede we him to doon amys.   720

(91)

In con[u]eniendo populos in vnum, et reges ut seruiant Domino.

In gaderynge of peplis in oon,
   And of kyngis God to serue,
To be stidefast as is the stoon,   F. 37 b.
   In his seruice þat we not s[w]erue,   If we are
The wey of truthe we schulde goon,   725   faithful in
   To trecchery we schulde not [t]erue,   His service,
And, if we dide þus euerichoon,   we shall be
   There schulde no care oure cumfort kerue.   happy.

724. So K.; MS. sterue.
726. So K.; MS. cerue.

(92)

Respondit ei in via virtutis sue : Paucitatem dier*um*
meor*um* nu*n*cia michi.

He answeride in þe wey of my3t,
 " Telle me þe lytilheed of my dayes."   730
Þus answeriþ ech a Cristen kny3t
 That 3eueþ no force of riche ara*y*es ;
For he þinkiþ how deep is di3t,
 To a-saye ech a man w*ith* scharpe asayes ;
He haldiþ to God his herte vpri3t,   735
 And feri[þ] him not of siche afrayes.

(93)

Ne reuoces me in dimidio dier*um* meor*um* ; *in* generacione[m] et gene*r*ac*i*o*n*em anni tui.

Ne calle me not in þe [halfundele]
 Of my dayes þoru-out þe 3heer,
For þei slyden as mydday meel,
 And passen as þe cloudis cleer.   740
There ys no surete [ne] no seel
 Of ma*n*nys lijf while he is heer ;
Therfore, Ihe*s*u, þat knowist me freel,
 Wisse me wha*n*ne I am in weer.

(94)

Inicio tu, Dom*i*ne, terram fundasti ; & ope*r*a manuu*m*
tuar*um* su*n*t celi.

For, Lord, þou bigu*n*ne þe grounde ;   745
 Thin handwerkis ben heuenes alle,
Al þis world, þ*at* is so rounde,
 Of creaturis grete and smalle.
Thou hast hem py*n*ned in a pou*n*de,
 Wiþ-oute warde of wou3 or walle,   750
And, while þou list, þou sauest he*m* sou*n*de
 And, wha*n*ne þou wilt, þei schulen dou*n* falle.

736. MS. fe*r*ida ; K. feryght. 737. *So* K. ; MS. myddil.
   741. *So* K. ; MS. of.

(95)

Ipsi peribunt, tu autem permanes ; | et omnes sicut
vestimentum veterascent.

Thei schulen peresche, but þou schalt dwelle,
　Alle schulen eelde liyk a clooþ,
Al vanyte þou schalt down felle,　　　　　　　755
　And make it leef þat now is looþ ;
For þere is no tunge that can telle
　What peyne it is to se þee wrooþ,
Whanne þou schalt close þe gates [of] helle,
　And curse[n] alle þat þidir gooþ.　　　　　760

All things pass away, but Thou remainest ; Thou wilt cast the wicked into Hell.

(96)

Et sicut oportorium mutabis eos, et mutabuntur ; tu
autem idem ipse es, & anni tui non deficient.

And þou shalt as a couerlyte
　Hem chaunge, and þei schulen chaungid be ;
But alwey þou art riȝt parfiȝte,
　Thi ȝeeris schulen not fayle þee ;
Þerfore whanne þou hast maad us qwyte　　765
　Thoru myȝt of inmortalyte,
Þanne schalt þou be al oure delyte
　To se þi myȝtful magiste.

All will change, but Thou remainest ; we shall rejoice in heaven in Thy glory.

F. 39.

(97)

Filij seruorum tuorum habitabunt ; & semen eorum in
seculum dirigetur.

Thi seruauntis sones schulen dwelle & dure,
　And in al þe world her seed schal sprede ;　　770
For ceertis þei ben not [v]nsure,
　That þee wil serue in word & deede.
Þerfore now, Ihesu, do þi cure,
　Ne dampne us not whanne we ben dede,
But, eer we passe, make us pure,　　　　　　775
　To þe lond of lijf [þat] þou us lede.

Thy servants shall flourish ; grant, Lord, that we may be saved !

753. permanes : s added above the line.
759. K. yate of.　　　　　　771. So K. ; MS. ensure.

(98)

D E profundis clamaui ad te, Domine ; Domine,
      exaudi vocem meam.

Fro dalis depe to thee I criede ;
    Lord, Lord, listne þe voys of me !
This depe prisoun þat I in abyde,
    Breke it up, Lord, for thy pyte !   780
Be þou my socour and my gyde,
    My goostely Lord, to whom I fle,
And lete oute of þin herte ryde
    That I haue doon aȝeyn[e]s þee.

(99)

Fiant aures tue intendentes in uocem deprecacionis
mee.

Late þin eeris be maad listnynge   785
    Vnto þe vois of my preyere,
For wel I woot þou hast likynge
    In man [þat] þou hast bouȝt so dere ;
Therfore, what euere I rede or synge,
    Listen it, Lord, wiþ louely chere,   790
And vouche saaf at myn askynge
    My conscience to clense and clere.

(100)

Si iniquitates obseruaueris, Domine, Domine, quis
sustinebit ?

If þou rewarde al wickidnesse,
    Lord, Lord, who schal susteyne ?
For, by þe lawe of riȝtwijsnesse,   795
    Eendelees þanne were oure peyne.
But euere we hope to þi goodnesse,
    Whanne þou schalt al þis world affreyne,
With mercy and wiþ myldenesse
    Thi riȝtful doom þou wilt restreyne.   800

784. K. agenis.   788. *So* K.

(101)

Quia apud te propiciacio est; & propter legem tuam
sustinui te, Domine.

For wiþ þee is forȝifnesse,
    I haue þee suffrid, Lord, for þi lawe,
Thi lawe schal al vnriȝt redresse,
    Was neuere seyd no soþir sawe ;
Therfore, whanne thou schalt bodies blesse,   805
And deede men out of her dennys drawe,
Ihesu, þat sauerist al swetnesse,
    Lete no feend oure goostis gnawe.

With Thee is forgiveness ; save us from the fiend at the last !

(102)

Sustinuit anima mea in uerbo eius ; sperauit anima
mea in Domino.

My soule haþ suffrid in his word,
    In God my goost haþ had his trist ;   810
For synne is scharp as knyues oord,
    And makiþ hem lame þat liggiþ in lust ;
Therfore, Ihesu, thou louely lord,
    þere I am roten, rubbe of þe rust,
Or I be brouȝt to schippis bord,   815
    To sayle in-to þe sale of dust.

I have trusted in God ; O deliver me from my sins before I die !

F. 40 b.

(103)

A custodia matutina usque ad noctem, speret Israel in
Domino.

Fro þe morn ward into þe nyȝt
    Lete Israel triste in God and trowen.
Israel bitokeneþ ech a wiȝt
    That God schal se and goostly knowen.   820
To þis ech Cristen man haþ riȝt,
    þat wole his strengþe wel bistowen ;
He may be sikir, as God haþ hiȝt,
    That heuene blisse schal be his owne.

By God's promise, the man who trusts Him shall win Heaven.

801. sustinui te *written as one word and divided by a stroke.*

(104)

Quia apud Dominum misericordia, & copiosa apud
eum redempcio.

For at oure Lord is greet mercy,   825
  And plenteuous raunsum is hym wiþ;
He payede for us his owne body,
  In foorme of breed boþe lyme and lith;
Ceertis for oure sake oonly
  He was feynt as fowen in frith,   830
So þat synful may sikirly
  At hym gete grace and grith.

(105)

Et ipse redimet Israel ex omnibus iniquitatibus eius.

And he schal bye[n] Israel
  Fro hise mysdeedis euerilkone,
Whanne we schal rise in flesch & felle,   835
  And efte be cloþid in blood and boone.
Thanne schal þe feend, þat is so felle,
  Fer be flemyd & alle oure foone,
And gode men schulen in heuene dwelle;
  God ȝeue us grace þat we so doone!   840

(106)

DOmine, exaudi oracionem meam. Auribus percipe
obsecracionem meam in ueritate tua, & ex|audi
me in tua iusticia.

Lord, listne þou myn orisoun,
  Wiþ eeris my preyer þou perseyue,
In soþfastnes þou heere my soun,
  And in þi riȝt þou it resseyue!
Ihesu, þat regnest in þi regyoun,   845
  For hir loue þat þee can [con]seyue,
Late neuere þe feend us drawe doun,
  Ne dreedful deuel us disseyue!

826. *Catch-words:* He payede.   846. *So* K.; MS. resseyue.

(107)

Et non intres in iudicium cum seruo tuo, quia non
iustificabitur in conspectu tuo [omnis uiuens].

Come not in doom with þi seruaunt,
    For no lijf schal be iustifyed   850
In þi siȝt, ne nouȝt [þ]e faunt
    That þis day first in cradil cried.
For us schal plete no seriaunt,
    Al sotilte schal ben a-spyed ;
So wel is hym þat kepiþ couena[un]t,   855
    For word and werk al schal be tryed.

Judge us not, for none can be justified before Thee.

(108)

Quia persecutus est inimicus meus animam meam,
humiliauit in terra [uitam meam].

For-whi myn enemy haþ pursued
    My soule, and lowide my lijf in lond,
For, [when] I myȝte synne haue eschewid,
    My wil to wi[r]k[e] wolde I not wond.   860
But, Lord Ihesu, þat art endewid
    Wiþ grace, þou brynge me out of boond,
And sende me grace to be vertued,
    So þat I may þe feend wiþstoond.

F. 42.

Satan pursues me ; but, Lord, give me grace to withstand him !

(109)

Collocauit me in obscuris, sicut mortuos seculi. Et
anxiatus est super [me spiritus meus ; in me turbatum est
cor meum].

He put me in [placis derk] to be,   865
    As þei þat in þis world ben dede ;
My goost was greeuyd vpon me,
    Astonyed was myn herte for drede.
This ilke sorowe anoon I se,
    Whanne I haue doon a deedly deede ;   870
Therfore, Ihesu ful of pytee,
    In þis myscheef me rule and rede !

I was sore oppressed for deadly sin ; Lord, direct me!

F. 42 b.

851. *So* K. ; MS. ne.   855. MS. couenāut.
859. *So* K.   860. *So* K. ; MS. wickidnis
865. MS. derk placis.   867. goost *altered from* grost.

(110)

Memor fui dier*um* antiquor*um*; meditatus s*um* in
omnib*us* op*er*ibus tuis; in factis manuu*m* tuar*um*
meditabar.

I remem-
bered how
Christ, be-
trayed by
Judas,
gathered his
flock.

I hadde mynde of dayes oolde,
  Of alle þi werkis I me biþouȝte,
How synfully þat Iudas soolde   875
  Hym þat [þis world w*ith* hondis] wrouȝt.
With greet penau*n*ce gaderide his foolde
  That scheparde þat oure soulis bouȝt;
Þe cu*m*fort of oure cares coolde,
  Of [C]rist it cam, for he it brouȝt.   880

(111)

Expandi manus meas ad te; anima mea sicut te*rr*a
sine aq*ua* tibi.

Grant me,
Lord, sor-
row for sin !

To þee myn hondis, Lord, I spradde;
  My soule is lijk lond watirlees;
I may not wepe, I am so badde,
  So bareyn and so sorowlees.
Sy*n*ne constreyneþ me ful sadde;   885

F. 43.

  Therfore I preye þe, prince of pees,
Helpe me þat I su*m*me teris hadde,
  That goostly fruyte [myȝte haue] encrees.

(112)

Uelociter exaudi me, Domine; defecit spiritus meus.

I have neg-
lected Thy
faith ; but
cast me not
away !

Listne, Lord, and heere me ȝerne;
  The goost of me forsoþe haþ failid,   890
For I haue ben ful looþ to lerne
  Þing þat myȝte me haue avayled;
But, Lord, þat openest þi posterne
  For hem þat for þee han trauaylid,
I hope þou wilt no bonde sperne,   895
  Þat is wiþ sorowe of sy*n*ne assayled.

876. *So* K.; MS. w*ith* hondis þis world.
880 *So* K.; MS trist.   888. *So* K.

(113)

Ne auertas faciem tuam a me, & similis ero descenden-
tib*us* *in* lacu*m*.

Thi face turne not me fro !
    I schal be lijk he*m* þat fallen in lake.
Þe da*m*pnyd men may wel sey so,
    That are bitauȝt þe feendis blake.   900
But lete me, Lord, be noon of þo ;
    Thinke how þou diedist for my sake,
And graunte me gr*a*ce, eer þat I go,
    Of my trespas amendis make.

Thou didst die for me ; let me not perish !

F. 43 b.

(114)

Auditam fac michi mane misericordiam tua*m*, q*uia* in
te sp*er*aui.

Thi m*er*cy make me heere a-morowe,   905
    For I haue had on þee myn hope.
Helpe þat I were out of [h]orowe,
    And alle þat þere-y*n*ne are lope.
Lord, þou suffridist schame & sorowe,
    And bled[dist] manye a blody drope ;   910
Fro goostli bondis þou me borowe,
    That I were out of synne crope.

For Thy Passion, rescue me from the bonds of sin !

(115)

Notam fac michi uiam i*n* qua ambulem, q*uia* ad te
leuaui a*n*i*m*am mea*m*.

Teche me þe way þat I schal weende,
    For I my soule to þee haue lift ;
Þis worldis welþe haþ [soone] an eende,   915
    And takiþ a-wey [a] ma*n*nys þrift.
Þerfore, Ih*es*u curteys and kynde,
    Whos herte was on cros [y]-clift,
Late neu*er*e feend oure paþis blende,
    Ne us bitraye neu*er*e eft !   920

The world passes away; let not the fiend betray us !

F. 44.

907. MS. borowe.   910. *So* K.   915. *So* K.
916. *So* K. ; MS. soone.   918. *So* K.

(116)

Eripe me de inimicis meis, Domine, ad te confugi;
doce me facere voluntatem [tuam, quia Deus meus
es tu].

Delyuere me, Lord, fro my foos felle !

For strengþe to þee fled am I ;

Teche me þi wille to fulfille,

For-whi þou art my God oonli.

Down myn enemyes þou felle ;   925

Resseyue me, Lord, to þi mercy,

That I may dreedlees in þee dwelle,

And þou, Lord, in me eendeleesly.

(117)

Spiritus tuus bonus deducet me in terram rectam.
Propter nomen tu[um, Domine, uiuificabis me, in equi-
tate tua].

Thi good goost, [Lord], schal me lede

Streiȝt in-to þe lond of riȝt,   930

And, for þi name in riȝtfulheede,

Thou schalt me make qwike & liȝt.

Þanne schal I dwelle[n] out of dreede

Where euere is day and neuere nyȝt,

For grisly goost schal þere noon grede   935

O[n] hem þat ben in blis[se] briȝt.

(118)

Educes de tribulacione animam meam; & in misericordia tua disperdes omnes inimicos meos.

My soule þou schalt brynge out of care,

Wiþ mercy my foo-men disp[arpl]ye,

And make þe deuel droupe & dare,

That he drawe me to no folye ;   940

And, God, þat I be not [maad] bare

Of alle goodnes þat I can aspie,

[Ȝit], ȝit, Lord, abyde and spare,

Þat I be amendid or I dye.

936. *So* K. ; MS. of.   938. *So* K. ; MS. disprauye.
941. *So* K.   943. MS. and.

(119)

Et perdes omnes qui tribulant animam meam, quoniam
ego seruus tuus sum.

And þou schalt lese hem that dissesen	945
My soule, for I serue thee ;	
Late no more vppon me resen	
þe goostes þat han greeued me ;	
Sende me grace thee to plesen,	
And vouche saaf, whanne doom schal be,	950
In-to þe kingdom of heuene me sey[s]en ;	
þus graunte me, God in Persoonys þre !	
Amen.	

F. 45.
Destroy
Thou my
enemies, and
grant that I
may have
my place in
Heaven !

V.

[LESSONS FROM THE DIRIGE.]

Parce michi, Domine.　　Leccio prima.

S Pare me, Lord ; forsoþe my dayes ben nouȝt. What
is man, þat þou magnifiest hym, or wherto settiste
þou þin herte towardis hym? þou visitist hym in þe
5 dawenynge, and sodeynli þou prouest hym. How long
sparist þou not me, ne suffrist þat I swolewe my spotil?
I haue synned ; what schal I do to þee, O þou keper of
men? | Whi hast þou sett me contrarye to þee, and I
am maad heuy to my-silf? Whi takist þou not awey
10 my synne, and wherfore berist þou not awey my wickidnesse? Lo now I slepe in poudir, and, if þou seke me
eerly, I schal not with-stonde.

Responsorium. I bileeue þat myn aȝeinbier lyueþ, and
I schal rise of þe erþe in þe laste day, and in my flesch I
15 schal se God my Saueour.

Ver. Whom I my-silf schal se, and noon oþer, and
myn iȝen schulen se hym.

And in my flesch I schal se God my Saueour.

Job vii.
16-21.

F. 45 b.

951. So K. ; MS. resseyuen,

Tedet animam meam vite mee.   Leccio ijᵃ.

Job x. 1–7.

IT anoieþ my soule of my lijf, and I schal leue my
speche aʒeins me, in bittirnesse I schal speke to my
soule.   I schal seye to God : Wil þou not dampne me.
Schewe to me whi þou wilt deeme me þus.   Wheþir it 5
F. 46.
þinke þee good if þou chaleu|ge and bere down me þe
werk of þin handis, and þou helpist þe counceyl of
wickide men ?   Wheþir fleischly iʒen ben to þee, or þou
seest as a man ?   Wheþer as dayes of men þi dayes, or þi
ʒeeris ben as mennys tymes, þat þou seeke my wickidnesse 10
and ransake my synne ?   And [wite] þou for I haue no
wickid þing doon, siþin þere is no man þat may ascape
fro þin hond.

R̶. Thow þat reisidist up aʒein Laʒar of þe monument stynkynge, þou, Lord, ʒeue hem reste and space of 15
forʒeuenesse.

Ver. He þat is to come to deeme qwike and deede,
and þe world bi fier.

Þou, Lord, ʒeue hem rest and space of forʒeuenesse.

Manus tue fecerunt me.   Leccio iijᵃ.   20

Job x. 8–12.

THyne hondis maden me and schopyn me al in cum-
pas, and so sodeynly þou castist me down.   Haue
F. 46 b.
mynde, I biseche þee, þat as myre þou hast maad | me,
and in-to poudir þou schalt aʒein lede me.   Ne hast þou
softid me as mylk and cruddidist me as chese ?   Wiþ 25
skyn and fleischis þou cloþidist me, wiþ boones and wiþ
senewes þou ioynedist me to-gydere, lijf and mercy þou
ʒaf me, and þi visitacioun haþ·kept my goost.

R̶. Lord, whanne þou comest to deeme þe erþe, where
schal I hyde me fro þe face of þi wraþþe ?   For I haue 30
synned riʒt myche in my lijf.

Ver. My trespasse I dreede, and bifore þee I am
a-schamyd.   Whanne þou comest to iuggement wil þou
not condempne me.

For I haue synned riʒt myche in my lijf.   35

Quantas habeo iniquitates. Leccio iiijᵃ.

A S grete wickidnessis and synnes, felonyes and trespassis, I haue, schewe þou me. Why hydist þou
þi face and deemest me þin enemy? Aӡein þe leef þat
is taken of þe wynd þou sche|wist [þi myӡt], and þe drye
stobil þou pursuest. þou wrytist forsoþe aӡeins me
bittirnessis, and þou wilt waaste me wiþ þe synnes of
my ӡouþe. þou hast sette my foot in stockis, and þou
hast kepte alle my by-paþis, and þow hast biholde þe
steppis of my feet, and I schal be wastid as rotenesse,
and as cloþing þat is eten of a moþþe.

R̰ᵐ. Wo to me, Lord, for I haue synned to myche in
my lijf. What schal I do, wrecche, whidir schal I fle
but to þee, my God? Haue mercy of me whanne þou
comest in þe laste day.

Ver. My soule is mykil troublid, but þou, Lord, be
helper þer-to.

Whanne þou comest in þe laste day.

Job xiii 23-28.

F. 47.

Homo natus de muliere. Leccio vᵃ.

M An born of a womman, lyuynge a schort tyme, is
fulfillid of al wickidnesse : which gooþ out as a
flour and is troden, and fleeþ as þe schadowe, and | dwelliþ
neuere in þe silue staat, and þou leetist þee worþi to
opene þin iӡen vpon sich oon, and lede hym wiþ þee
in-to þe iuggement. Who may make hym clene þat is
conseyued of vnclene seed? Wheþir þou þat art aloone?
Schorte are a mannys dayes, and þe noumbre of hise
moneþis is at þee, þou hast sette hise teermys þat mown
not passe. Go awey þerfore a litil fro hym, þat he reste
til þe day desirid come, and as of a marchaunt þe dayes
of hym.

R̰ᵐ. Haue no mynde of my synnes, Lord, whanne
þou comest to deeme þe world by fier.

Ver. Lord my God, dresse my wey in þi siӡt.

Whanne þou comest to deeme þe world by fier.

Job xiv. 1-6.

F. 47 b.

Quis michi hoc tribuat vt inferno protegas.
Leccio vjᵃ.

Job xiv.
13–16.
F. 48.

WHo ȝeueþ to me þat þou defende me in helle, and
þat þou hyde me til þi|wraþþe be passid, and þat
þou sette to me a tyme'in whilk þou schalt bere recorde   5
of me ? Trowist þou þat a deed man schal lyue aȝeyn ?
Alle þe dayes in þe whiche I now fiȝte, I abyde til þe
tyme þat my goostly liknesse come. þou schalt calle
me, and I schal answere to þee ; to þe werk of þin hondis
þou schalt putte oute þi riȝt half. þou forsoþe hast   10
noumbrid my goyngis, but spare my synnes.

℞. Lord, aftir my deede wil þou not deeme me.
Noþing worþi haue I doon in þi siȝt, þerfore I praye þi
mageste þat þou, God, do awey my wickidnesse.

Ver. Moore-ouere waysche me, God, of myn vnriȝt-   15
wijsnesse, and of my trespasse clense þou .me, for to þee
aloone I haue synned.

þerfore I praye þi maieste þat þou, God, do awey my
wickidnesse.

F. 48 b.

Spiritus meus|attenuabitur, dies mei. Leccio vijᵃ.   20

Job xvii.
1–3, 11–15.

MY goost schal be maad þinne, my dayes schulen be
schortid, and oonly a biryel ouer-bileueþ to me.
I haue not synned, and myn iȝe dwelliþ in bittirnesse.
Delyuere me, Lord, and sette me bisidis þee ; and whos
hond þat þou wilt, fiȝte aȝeins me ! My dayes are passid,†   25
my þouȝtis are waa[s]tid, turmentynge myn herte. þei
turnyd nyȝt to day, and thanne aftir derknesse I hope
liȝt. If I susteyne, helle is myn hows, in derknes I
haue beddid my bed. I seyde to rotennesse : þou art
my fadir and my modir, and to wormes I seyde : þou   30
art my sistir. Where is þanne myn abidynge and my
pacience ? þou art, Lord my God !

℞ᵐ. The dreede of deep troublide me, synnynge ech

25. MS. passid, *written on a slightly longer word which has been
erased.*
26. MS. waaftid.

day and not repentynge, for | in helle is no redempcyoun. F. 49.
Haue mercy on me, God, and saue me.
Ver. God, in þi name make me saaf, and in þi vertu
delyuere me.
5 For in helle is no redempcioun.

Pelli mee consumpt[i]s. Leccio octaua.

MY mouth cleuede to my skyn, þe fleisch wastid, Job xix.
20-27.
and al oonly þe lippis are left a-boute my teeth.
Haue ruþe on me, haue ruþe on me, namely 3e my
10 frendis, for þe hond of oure Lord haþ touchid me. Whi
pursue 3e me as God, and 3e ben fulfillid wiþ my fleschis?
Who schal 3eue to me þat my wordis ben writen? Whoo
schal 3eue to me þat þei ben grauen in a book wiþ a
poyntel of irun and in a plate of leed, oþir þat þei be
15 grauen in a flynt wiþ a chisel? I woot forsoþe þat myn
a3eynbier lyueþ, and in þe laste day I am for to ryse fro
þe erþe, and eft | I schal be lappid in my skyn, and in F. 49 b.
my flesch I schal se God my Saueour, whom I my-silf
schal se, and myn i3en are to byholde on hym, and noon
20 oþir. Þis is myn hope put up in my bosum.
R̂. Lord, 3eue hem rest wiþ-outen eende, and þe li3t
þat euere lastiþ li3tne to hem.
Ver. Thou þat reridist La3ar fro þe monument stink-
ynge, 3eue to hem, Lord, reste.
25 And the li3t þat euere lasteþ li3tne to hem.

Quare de vulua eduxisti me. Leccio ixᵃ.

WHy led[d]ist þou me out of þe wombe? Wolde Job x.
18-22.
God þat I hadde be fordoon, þat noon i3e hadde
seen me! Þanne hadde I ben as þou[3] I hadde not ben,
30 fro þe wombe boren to þe biriel. Wheþir þe schort-
nesse of my dayes schal not ben eendid in schort? Late
me, Lord, þat I weyle a litil while my sorowe, or þat | I F. 50
go, and turne not a3eyn, to þe derk erþe, keuerid wiþ þe
derk cloude of þe deep, þe lond of wrecchidnesse and of

1. *Catch-word* in. 6. MS. consumptus.

derkenesse, where is schadowe of deeþ and noon ordir,
but euerlastynge [o]rrour wiþ-in dwellynge.

§ Delyuere me, Lord, of eendelees deeþ, in þat dreedful
day, whanne þat þe heuenys schulen be stirid fro þe
erþe, whanne þou schalt come to iuge þe world by   5
fier.

§ That day schal be a day of wraþþe, and ful of
myscheef and of wrecchidnesse, a greet day and riȝt
bittir.

Whanne þou schalt come to iuge þe world by fier.   10

§ What schal I þanne, moost wrecche, what schal I
seye or what schal I do, whanne I schal schewe no
goodnesse bifore so greet a iuge?

Whanne þou schalt come to iuge þe world by fier.

F. 50 b.   § Now Crist, we aske þee, ha|ue mercy, we biseke þee. 15
Þou þat cam to byen us þat were loren, wil þou not
dampne hem þat þou hast bouȝt.

Whanne þou schalt come to iuge þe world by fier.

Ver. Brennynge soulis wepen wiþ-outen eende, walkinge
by derknesse, and þei seyen echoone of þo: Wo! Wo! 20
Wo! how grete are þese derkenesses þere we go!

Ver. Schapper of alle þingis, God þat foormedist me of
þe sliym of þe erþe, and wondirly wiþ þin owne blood
hast bouȝt us, if my bodi rotye now, þou schalt make it
arise of þe sepulcre in þe day of doom. Heere me, heere 25
me, þat þou comaunde my soule be put in þe bosum of
Abraham þi patriark.

Whanne þou schalt come to iuge þe world by fier.

Rȝ^m. Delyuere me, Lord, of þe weyes of helle, þou þat
brake þe gatis ʽof bras, and visitist helle, and ȝaf liȝt to 30
F. 51.   hem, þat þei þat we|ren in peynes myȝten se þee, criynge
and seiynge: Þou art come, oure aȝeynbier. Delyuere
me, Lord, of þe weyes of helle. Reste þei in pees.
Amen.

2. MS. errour.

VI

[A SONG OF MERCY AND JUDGMENT]

(1)

THere is no creatour but oon,
   Maker of ech a creature,
Oon God, and euere oon,
For þre in oon alwey endure.
To þat Lord we make oure moone,   5
In whom is al cumfort and cure ;
To þinke how frel[e] we ben echoon !
þis world ne is but hard auenture ;
   For whose moste þer-ynne [e]s sure
   Sunnest [schal he be] schamyd and schent ;   10
   Whanne þou þis world wiþ fier schalt pure,
   Do mercy bifore þi iuggement.

There is but one God, to Whom we pray for mercy before the Day of Judgment.

(2)

§ We asken mercy or þou deeme,
Leste þou dampne þat þou hast i-wrouȝt.
What ioye were it þe deuel to qweme,   15
To ȝeue hym þat þou hast bouȝt ?
And, of þi siȝt if þou us fleeme,
We weren but lost riȝt as nouȝt ;
Now make us lijk siche as [þe]e seeme,
In loue and dreede þou sette oure þouȝt.   20
   For synne us haþ so þoru-souȝt,
   þere is no trist in oure entent ;
   Vnto acount or we ben brouȝt,
   Do mercy bifore thi iuggement.

Thou hast made and redeemed us ; keep us true to Thee !

F. 51 b.

(3)

§ For þou hast biden us aske and haue ;   25
That ȝeueþ us cumfort for to calle ;
And þou hast ordeyned, [man] to saue,
† Mercy aboue þi werkis alle.

Thou hast redeemed us ; give us grace to resist the devil !

7. MS. frely.   9. MS. assure.   10. MS. is.   19. MS. we.
27. MS. for.   28. MS. man mercy. *The stop marking the end
of a line is after* saue.

WHEATLEY MS.   F

Also þin herte blood for us þou gaue,
To make us fro þat eer weren pralle ; 30
Late neuere þe deuel þat soule depraue
That wayschen was in holy walle.
    Oure fleisch is freele þat makiþ us falle ;
    Wiþ grace we a-ryse and schulen repente,
    And þus we hope þat we schalle 35
    Haue mercy bifore þi iuggement.

(4)

§ We asken mercy of al þing,
Thou art kynde in ech degre,

F. 52.
For þou gaue us wiþ stoones beyn|ge,

Thou gavest us being, growth, life, understand-ing and faith, and didst redeem us.

And wiþ þi spiryt endowid us fre ; 40
With trees þou gaue us growynge,
Wiþ beestis, feelynge lijf haue we,
Wiþ aungels, vndirstondynge.
Wiþ bileeue weddid vnto þee,
    And wiþ þi blood bou3t be we ; 45
    3i[t] we ben fals and necligent,
    That we mowen neuere clymbe ne fle
    Þi mercy ne thy iuggement.

(5)

Therefore we commend our souls to Thee, in life and death.

§ Wherfore oure soulis & oure lijf
Into þin hondis we bitake, 50
Out of temptacyoun and strijf
To saue us whanne we slepe or wake.
Now, Ihesu, for þi woundes fijf,
And also for þi modris sake,
Þe deuel awey fro us þou drijf 55
Whanne deeþ schal hise maystryes make.
    Thou seydist þou woldist us nou3t forsake
    Whanne þou on rode were al torent ;
    Agayn þi doom we crye and qwake,
    Do mercy bifore þi iuggement. 60

34. we *written above the line.* 46. MS. 3if.

(6)

§ And, ȝeue þou deeme us riȝtfully,
Ȝeue mercy þe execucyoun,
And, if we haue seruyd þee vnkyndely,
Take heede to oure entencyoun.
We ȝeelde us synful and sory, 65
Wiþ knowleche and contricioun;
Oure baptym and þi mercy
We take to oure proteccyoun.
   Bileeue is oure saluacyoun
   By lawe of þi comaundement; 70
   Now, Crist, putte al [þi] passyoun
   Bitwixe us and þi iuggement.
           AMEN.

F. 52 b.

Judge us with mercy; we repent of our sins, and trust to Thy Passion in our last Judgment.

VII

[A PRAYER FOR MERCY]

(1)

A Lmyȝti God, maker of heuene,
   Eyr and erþe, watir and wynde,
To þee I calle wiþ mylde steuene,
   That flesch and blood took of mankynde.
Out of synne my soule vnbynde 5
   Þat for me diedist on þe tre;
To ryken I am ful fer bihynde,
   But, Ihesu, þou haue mercy on me.

God, Who madest all things, and didst redeem me, have mercy on me!

(2)

§ If I schulde riȝtwijs rikenynge make
   Fro þe tyme þat I was bore, 10
Þanne woldist þou veniaun|ce take,
   Þanne were I lost [for] euermoore.
Thou hast ordeyned salue for elke a soore,
   And mercy soulis leche to be;
That þou hast bouȝt late neuere be lore, 15
   But, Ihesu, þou haue mercy on me.

F. 53.

By justice I should be lost, but save me through Thy mercy!

71. MS. oure.

(3)

Grant me,
Lord, the
mercy Thou
hast promis-
ed to all
who ask it !

§ Wiþ-outen þee no man haþ myȝt,
    Pore ne riche, lowe ne hiȝe ;
þinke þou hast mercy bihiȝt
    To alle þat it askiþ mekely.   20
Wiþ woful herte and wepinge iȝe
    I ȝeelde me, Lord, þus vnto þee,
And for my mys mercy I crye ;
    Now, Ihesu, haue mercy on me.

(4)

Though I
have sinned
grievously,
remember
Thou hast
redeemed
me, and ·
have mercy
on me !

§ Thouȝ synne my soule fro þee haue twynnyd,   25
    þinke how dere þou hast [me] bouȝt ;
And, if my freel fleisch haue synned,
    Dere Lord, I forsook þee nouȝt.
Ful wickidly eft haue I wrouȝt,
    Vnchast and out of charyte   30
In word, in wille, in werk, in þouȝt ;
    Now, Ihesu, haue þou mercy on me.

(5)

§ Lord, to þee þus I me ȝelde
    Wiþ knowleche and contricioun ;

F. 53 b.
I repent my
sins ; grant
Thou me
space to
amend
them !

Of alle | my synnes in [y]out[h] and celde,   35
    [Grant], riȝtwijs God, remyssyoun
And space of satisfaccyoun ;
    As þou art prynce of al pytee,
On my beere or I be bo[un],
    Ihesu, haue mercy on me.   40

(6)

Jesus, Sav-
iour, help
me ; Mary,
pray for me !

§ Thy riȝt name þat is Ihesu,
    That is to seye, oure saueour.
þanne I aske it as dewe,
    Of þin help and socour
Now sende me help fro heuene tour,   45
    þat liȝtist in a mayden fre ;
Now, Marye mayde, swete flour,
    Praye Ihesu haue mercy on me.

35. MS. þouȝt.   39. MS. bore.

(7)

§Now mercy, I am in wille no moore

Fro hennys forth to [do] trespace,   50

Now mercy, þat I be not loore,

Now mercy, Lord, and graunte me grace

Þat I may se þi swete face

Th[er] þou art God in Trynyte,

And in heuene to haue a place ;   55

Now, Ih*esu*, þou haue mercy on me.

I firmly purpose amendment ; grant that I may see Thy Face in Heaven, and have mercy on me !

A*MEN.*

VIII

[GOD'S COMPLAINT]

(1)

THis is Goddi*s* owne compleynt

    Fro Man to man þ*at* he haþ [b]ouȝt,

And þus he seith to hem [a]teynt :

" Myn owne peple, what haue I wrouȝt,

[Þat thou] art to me so feynt,   5

And I þi loue so fer haue souȝt ?

In þin answer no þing þou peynt

To me, for-whi I knowe þi þouȝt. ,

    Haue I not do al þat me ouȝt ?

    Haue I left ony þing bihynde ?   10

    Whi wrappist þou me ? I greue þee nouȝt.

    Why artow to þi Lord vnkynde ?

F. 54.

God's complaint : O My people, what have I done to thee ?

(2)

I souȝte þi loue, and þ*at* was seene

Wha*n*ne I made þee lijk to me ;

On erþe my werkis boþe q*ui*ke & greene   15

I putte hem vndir þi pouste ;

Fro Farao þat was so kene

Of Egypt I delyueride þee,

I killide hym and hise bidene ;

The Reed[e] See atwynne to fle   20

I first made thee ; I delivered thee from Pharaoh, and brought thee across the Red Sea.

F. 54 *b.*

54. MS. that.   2. MS. wrouȝt.

3. MS. enteynt.   5. MS. thou þat.

I bad, þat drye it schulde be ;
I ceesside þe watir and þe wynde ;
I brouȝte þee ouere and maad þee fre ;
Whi art þou to þi freend vnkynde ?

(3)

I led thee
through the
wilderness;
I became
Man and
died for
thee.

And fourti ȝeer in wildirnesse   25
Wiþ auugels foode I þee fedde ;
In-to þe lond of greet richesse
To schewe þee loue, þere I þee ledde ;
To do þee moore of kyndenesse,
To take þi kynde I no-þing dredde,   30
I lefte my myȝt and took mekenesse,
Myn herte blood for þee I bledde.
    Thi soule to saue, my lijf I ledde ;
    I boonde my-silf þee to vnbynde ;
    Þus wiþ my wo þi nedis I spedde ;   35
    Whi art þou to þi Lord vnkynde ?

(4)

For the I ordeynede Paradys ;
Fre wille was þin affeffement ;

F. 55.
I gave thee
free will,
and thou
didst obey
Mine enemy.

How myȝtist þou me moore dispise
Þanne breke my owne comaundement,   40
And synne in seuene maner wyse,
And to myn enemy so soone assent ?
He put þee doun, þou myȝtist not rise ;
Þi strenkþe, þi witt away was went.
    Pore, nakid, schamyd and schent,   45
    That frendschip myȝte þou noon fynde
    But me þat on þe rode was rent ;
    Why art þou to þi Lord vnkynde ?

(5)

I am thy
Friend ; re-
turn to Me,
and I will
forgive thee,
as I did St.
Mary Mag-
dalene and
St. Thomas.

Man, I loue þee ; whom louest þou ?
I am þi freend ; whi woltow feyne ?   50
I forȝaf, and þou me slouȝ ;
Who haþ departid oure loue in tweyne ?
Turne to me, biþinke þee how
Þou hast goon mys, come hoom aȝeyne,
And þou schalt be as welcome now   55
As he þat neuere dide foreyne.

Wayte how dide Marye Maudeleyne,
And what [I] seyde to Thomas of Ynde.
I grauntide þee blis, whi louest þou peyne?
Whi art þou to þi Lord vnkynde?   60

F. 55 b.

(6)

Off a freend þe fairist preef
Is loue wiþ drede and not displese;
Was neuere no þing to me so leef
As mankynde þat no þing may pese †.
I suffride for þi synnes repreef,   65
In hiȝ heuene þi soule to cese;
I was hangid as a þeef;
Þou didist þe dede, I hadde þe dissese.
    Þou canst me neiþer þanke ne plese,
    Ne do good deede, ne haue me in mynde;   70
    I am þi leche in þi dissese;
    Whi art [þou] to þi freend vnkynde?

I have proved My love by dying for thy sins.

(7)

Unkynde, for þou killidist þi Lord,
And euery day þou woundist me newe;
Þouȝ we ben brouȝt to oon a-coord,   75
In couenaunt-briche þou art vntrewe,
And redy aȝeyn to resoort
To folowe vicis and fle vertuwe;
Al ribaudrie þou canst repoort;
Wo is hym þi wraþþe may not eschewe.   80
    Þou art redy to pursuwe
    The pore peple wiþ sleyȝtis blynde;
    Þou schalt out of þis world remewe,
    By-cause þou art to þi freend vnkynde.

But thou ever grievest Me by remaining in sin.

F. 56.

(8)

The deuel temptide me neuere but þrie,   85
And þou [me temptist] fro day to day;
Wiþ cursyng aftir veniaunce to crye,
To stire [my] wraþþe þou wilt assay.

Thou temptest My anger continually; thou wouldest betray Me.

58. MS. he.   64. MS. plese.
86. MS. temptist me.   88. MS. wiþ.

Þou woldist, and ony wolde me bye,
Wel wors þan Iudas me bitray ;   90
At my werkis þou hast envye ;
Wele neiþer wo may þee noon pay.
    And þou me my3tist, as I þee may,
    Wel bittirly þou woldist me bynde ;
    I for3af, and þou seidist nay ;   95

F. 56 b.   Thus am I freend and þou vnkynde.

                    (9)

I have
bought thy
love with
My life, and
thou deniest
Me thy
homage.
I haue bou3t þi loue ful dere.
Vnkynde, whi forsakist þou myn?
I 3af þee [myn] herte and blood in fere.
Vnkynde, whi woldist þou not 3eue me þin ?   100
Thou art an vnkynde homagere,
And with my foo þou makist þi fyn,
And seruest me with feble chere,
To hym þin herte wole holly enclyn.
    And I am lord of blisse and pyne,   105
    And al[le] þing[is] may lese and bynde ;
    A3eyns þee my gatys I wil tyne
    Al þe while þou art vnkynde.

                    (10)

Remember
that thou
art in My
hand, and
turn to Me.
Man, biþinke þee what þou arte,
Fro whens þou cam, and whidir þou art boun ; 110
If þou þis day be hool and quarte,
To-morowe I may put þee doun.
Lete mylde and mekenes melte þin herte ;
Þou ruwe vpon my passyoun,
F. 57.   My wyde woundis depe and smerte,   115
Wiþ cros[se], naylis, spere, and coroun.
    Late drede and good discrecyoun
    Thyn herte holly vp to [me] seende ;
    Þou hast fyue wyttis and resoun,
    And, if þou wilt, þou may be kynde."   120

                114. *Catch-words* My wyde.

(11)

A, Lord ! wi*th* þee we wolen not plete,
But, as þou seist, it is and was ;
We haue disserued helle heete,
But now we ȝelde us vnto þi gras.
We wolen bowe, and þou schalt bete   125
And chastise us for oure trespas ;
Late mercy for us so now entrete
Þ.it neue*r*e no feendis oure soulis chas.
   A, blisful Lady, fayre of fas,
   Helpe, for we ben fer bihynde ;   130
   Or wepynge we mown seye, " Allas,
   Why were we to oure freend vnkynde ? "
           A*men*.

Man's answer : Lord, we have sinned ; have mercy on us ; Mary, help us.

IX
To God

G Od, þat madist al þing of nouȝt,
   And wi*th* þi *pr*ecious blood us bouȝt,
   Mercy, helpe, and grace !
As þou art ve*rr*y God and Man,
And of þi syde þi blood ran,   5
   Forȝeue us oure trespáce !

Þe world, oure flesch, þe feend oure fo,
Makiþ us mys-þinke, mys-speke, mys-do ;
   Al þus we falle in blame ;
Of alle oure syn*n*es lasse and moore,   10
Swete I*h*e*sus*, us ruweþ soore ;
   Mercy for þin holy name !

O God, forgive us the sins to which the world, the flesh and the devil have tempted us

X
To oure Lady

M Arye, Goddis modir dere,
   Socoure & helpe us while we be*n* he*re*,
   Gouerne, wisse, and rede ;
As þou art modir, mayden, and wijf,
Clense us fro synne and grau*n*te good lijf,   5
   And helpe us in oure nede !

*Mary, Virgin and Moth*e*r, help us.*

XI

To Seynt Iohn

Saint John,
beloved of
our Lord,
intercede for
us.

S Eynt Iohn, for grace þou craue
   Þat of his mercy he wole us saue,
     As þou nexst hym were boren [on] b[r]este ;
And whanne we schulen fro hens weende,
Thou gete us grace to make good eende,   5
     In heuene blis wiþ hym to reste !
      AMEN.

XII

[HYMN FROM THE *SPECULUM CHRISTIANI*]

Mary, Virgin
and Mother,
protect and
help me ;

M Arye modir, wel þee be !
   Marye m[ayden], þinke on me !
Modir and mayde was neuere noon
To-gydere, Lady, but þou aloone.
Ma[rye] modir, mayden clene,   5
Schilde me to-day fro sorowe & tene.
Marye, out of synne helpe þou me

For thy Five
Joys,
And oute of dette for charyte.
Marye, for þi ioyes fyue,

F. 58 b.
Helpe me to lyue in clene lyue.   10

And for thy
tears by the
Rood.
For þe teeris þou weptist vndir þe rode,
Sende me grace of lynes foode,
Wherewiþ [I] may me cloþe and feede
And in truþe my lijf lede.

Help me and
all mine !
Helpe me, Lady, and al myne,   15
And schilde us alle fro helle pyne ;
Schilde us alle fro wordli schame
And fro al[le] wickid fame ;
Schilde us fro vilanye
And fro al wickid cumpanye.   20
Swete Lady, mayden mylde,

Protect me
from the
fiend !
Aȝeyn þe feend[e] þou me schilde ;
Þat þe feend me neuere dere,
Swete Lady, þou me were

2. MS. modir.   5. MS. mayden.   13. MS. me.

Boþe bi day and by ny3t,   25
Dere Lady, fair and bri3t.
For my freendis I bidde þee   *I pray to thee for my friends,*
That þei [mut amendid] be
Boþe to soule and to lijf,   *F. 59.*
Marye, for þi ioyes fijf.   30
For my foo-men I bidde also   *and for my enemies,*
That I and þei may so do
þat I ne þei in wrappe dye,
Swete Lady, I þee preye.
[And] þo þat ben in good[e] lijf ;   35   *for those who are in grace,*
Marye, for þi ioyes fijf,
Swete Lady, þere-ynne hem holde,
Be þei 3onge or be þei oolde ;
And þo þat ben in deedly synne,   *and for those in deadly sin.*
Ne late hem neuere dye þere-ynne.   40
Swete Lady, þou hem rede
That þei amende her mysdede ;
Marye, for þi ioyes alle,
Ne late hem neuere in synne falle.   *May I receive the*
Preye þi sone, heuene kyng,   45   *last Sacraments at my death, and enjoy eternal bliss.*
Sende me schrift, housel, & good eendyng.
Sende me, Lady, sich grace
In heuene blis to haue a place.   *F. 59 b.*
Marye, as I triste now to þee,
These preyers þou graunte me,   50
And helpe me to haue þat ilk blisse
That neuere [more] schal [ne] mysse.

AMEN.

Pater noster. Aue Maria. Credo in Deum.

28. MS. amendid mut.   35. MS. for.

XIII

[LIFE OF ADAM AND EVE]

**Here bigy𝑛neþ a tretys of Adam and Eue, oure
former fadir & modir, how þei weren maad,
whe𝑟e & where-of, how þei offendiden God, &
what penau𝑛ce þei suffriden he𝑟e pe𝑟fore, how
manye sones & dou3t𝑟i𝑠 þei hadden, & how longe 5
þei lyueden i𝑛 þis world, & of her eende.**

The creation of Man.

F. 60.

NOw takiþ hede þat, wha𝑛ne oure Lord God hadde
maad heuene [and erþe] and alle þe ourne-
mentis of he𝑚, God say þat þei weren gode, and | seyde :
" Make we man to oure ymage and liknesse, and be 10
he souereyn to þe fischis of þe see and to þe volatils of
heuene and to þe vnresonable beestis of erþe and to ech
creature & to ech reptile which is moued on þe erþe."
And God made of nou3t a man to his ymage and liknesse ; God made of nou3t a man to þe ymage of God ; 15
God made of nou3t hem male and female. And God
blesside hem & seyde : " Encreesse 3e & be 3e multiplied,
and fille 3e þe erþe and make 3e it soget, and be 3e
lordis to þe fischis of þe see and to þe volatyls of heuene
and to alle lyuynge beestis þat ben vpon erþe." And 20
God seyde : " Lo, I haue 3ouu𝑛 to 3ou ech eerbe berynge
seed vpo𝑛 erþe and alle trees þat han in hem-silf seed
i𝑛 her kynde, þat þo be in-to mete to 3ou and to alle
lyuynge beestis upon erþe and to ech brid of heuene

F. 60 b

and to alle þingis þat ben | mouyd on erþe and in which 25
is a lyuynge soule, þat þo haue · to ete." And it was
doon so, and God say alle þingis whiche he made, and
þo weren ful gode (Genesis j°). § The Lord God þa𝑛ne
foormede man of þe slij𝑚 of þe erþe and spiride in-to þe
face of him an entre of breeþ of lijf, and maad is man 30

Adam was made in Bethlehem.

into a soule 3euynge lijf. § Adam was maad in þe same
place of oure Lord God where þat Ihesu Crist was boru𝑛
ynne, þat is, in þe cytee of Bethleem, which is in þe
myddil of þe erþe ; and þere, of foure corners of þe

world, Adam body was maad. § And auₙgels brouȝten
þat erþe fro þo foure parties, þe whiche auₙgels ben
Mychael, Gabriel, Rafael, and Uryél. And þe erþe þat
þese auₙgels brouȝten was briȝt & schynynge as þe
5 sunne, and þat erþe was brouȝt out of foure floodis, þat is
to seye, Geon, Phison, Tygris, and Eufrates. § Thanne is
man lijk to þe ymage of | God maad, and God blew in his   F. 61.
face enspirynge of lijf, þat is to seye, his soule. § So as
he was maad of foure parties of þe erþe, also of foure
10 maner of wyndis he was enspirid. § Thanne oure Lord,
whanne Adam was maad, hadde ȝeue him no name; and   The naming of Adam.
þanne he seyde to þe foure auₙgels þat þei schuldeₙ
seche hym a name. § And Miȝhel wente forþ in-to þe
eest, and þere he say þe sterre þat hiȝte Annocoluₙ, and
15 he took þe firste lettre þerof. § And Rafael wente forþ
in-to þe south, and foond þe sterre of þe south þat hiȝte
Dysis, and he took þe first lettre þere-of. § And
Gabriel wente in-to þe north, and foond þere þe sterre of
þe north þat hiȝte Arthos, and he took þe firste lettre
20 þerof. § Þanne wente Vriel in-to þe west, and foond
þere þe sterre of þe west þat hiȝte Mensembryon, and he
took þe firste lettre þerof. § The|se lettris weren   F. 61 b.
brouȝt to oure Lord, and he bad Vriel reden hem, and
he radde hem, and seyde, "Adám," and oure Lord sayde,
25 "So schal his name be callid." **Versus : Annotele dedit**
A, Disis D, A contulit Arthos, M Mensembrion;
collige, fiet [Adam]. And ȝe schulen vndirstonde
þat Adam was maad of eiȝte þingis. O partye was of þe   Adam was made of eight things.
sliym of þe erþe, where-of his flesch was; and þere-of he
30 is slouȝ. § Anoþer partye was of þe see, where-of his
blood was; and þere-of he is couetous and bisy. § Þe
þridde partye was of stoonys of þe erþe; and þerfore
he is hard and bittir. § The fourþe partye was of þe
cloudis, where-of ben hise þinkyngis wrouȝt; and þere-
35 of he ys leccherous. § The fifþe partye was of þe
wynd, where-of is maad his breeþ; and þerof he is liȝt.
§ The sixte partye was of þe sunne, and þerof ben hise

27. fiet *has been added in the margin by the same hand. There
is not room for* Adam.
35. was *added above the line.*

F. 62. iȝen; and þerof he is fair and | cleer. § The seueþe
partye is of þe liȝt of þe world, where-of he is maad
glad; and þere-of he haþ his vndirstondyng. § The
eiȝtþe partye is of þe Holy Goost, and þerof is mannys
soule; and þerof ben þese holy profetis and alle Goddis   5
children. § Forsoþe þe Lord God plauntide Paradys of
delyte fro þe bigynnyng, in þe which he sette man
whanne he hadde foormyd hym. And þe Lord God
brouȝte forþ of þe erþe ech tre fair in siȝt and swete to
ete, also þe tre of lijf in þe myddil of Paradys,† and a   10
tre of knowynge good and yuel. § Thanne þe Lord

Adam is put
in Paradise. God took man and putte hym in Paradys of delyte, þat
he schulde worche and kepe it; and he comaundide to
hym, seiynge: "Of ech tre of Paradys ete; of þe tre
of knowynge good and yuel ete þou not; and what   15

F. 62 b. euere | day þou etist þerof, wiþ deep þou schalt dye."
§ The Lord God forsoþe seyde: "It is not good to man
to be aloone; make we to hym an help lijk to him."
§ The Lord God foormede of þe moist erþe alle þingis of
þe erþe hauynge soule and al volatiyl of heuene; þe   20
Lord God brouȝte hem to Adam, þat he schulde se what
he schulde clepe hem. Al þing forsoþe of soule lyuynge,
aftir þe kynde and þe propirte of it he ȝaf it name, and
riȝt as Adam clepide hem, sich is þe name of hem; but
to Adam forsoþe was not founden an helper lijk to hym. 25

The making
of Eve. §Thanne sente þe Lord sleep in-to Adam; and, whanne
he was a-slepe, he took oon of hise ribbis and fillid flesch
for it. And þe Lord God edifyede þe rib which he took
of Adam in-to a womman, and brouȝte hir to Adam.
§ Thanne Adam seyde: "Þis is now a boon of my 30

F. 63. boonys and flesch of my flesch; þis schal be | clepid
mannys deede, for sche is taken of man." Wherfore a
man schal forsake his fadir and modir, and schal drawe
to his wijf; and two schulen be in o flesch. § Eiþir forsoþe of hem was nakid, þat is, Adam and his wijf, and 35

The temp-
tation and
fall of man. þei schameden not (Genesis iijº). § But þe addir was
feller þan ony lyuers on erþe þe whiche þe Lord God
made. Þe which seyde to þe womman: "Whi comaun-

---

10. MS. *adds* and took man and put hym in paradys.

dide God to ȝou þat ȝe schulden not ete of ech tre of
Paradys?" To whom answeride þe womman : "Of þe
fruyt of þe trees þat ben in Paradys we eten, but of þe
fruyt of þe tre þat is in þe myddis of Paradys comaun-
5 dide us God þat we schulden not ete, and þat we
schulden not touche it, leste perauenture we dyen."
§ Forsoþe þe addir seyde to þe womman : "Þoru deeþ
ȝee schulen not dye. God forsoþe woot þat in | what   F. 63 b.
euere day ȝe eten þerof, ȝoure iȝen schulen ben openyd,
10 and ȝe schulen be as goddis, knowynge good and yuel."
§ Thanne þe womman say þat þe tre was good and swete
for to ete, and fair to þe iȝen, and delytable in þe siȝt;
and sche took of þe fruyt of it, [and eet], and ȝaf to hir
man, þe which eet; and þe iȝen of boþe ben openyd.
15 § And whanne þei knewen hem-silf to be nakid, þei
sewiden to-gydere leuys of fyge trees· and maden hem
brechis. § And whanne þei herden þe vois of þe Lord
goynge in Paradys [in] þe schynynge aftir mydday,
Adam and his wijf hidden hem fro þe face of þe Lord
20 God in þe myddil of þe trees of Paradys. And þe Lord
God clepide Adam and seyde to hym, "Where artow?" ;
which seyde : "Þi voys I herde in Paradys, and I dredde
þere-þoru þat I | was nakid, and I hidde me." To whom   F. 64.
seyde þe Lord : "Who forsoþe schewide þee þat þou
25 were nakid, but þat þou eet of þe tre of the which I
comaundide þee þat þou schuldist not ete?" And Adam
seyde : "Þe womman þat þou ȝauest felawe to me, ȝaf
to me of þe tre, and I eet." And þe Lord seyde to þe
womman : "Whi didist þou þat?" Þe which answeride :
30 "Þe addir bigylide me, and I eet." And þe Lord God
seyde to þe serpent : "For þou hast do þis þing, þou
schalt be cursid among alle þe soule-hauers and beestis
of þe erþe; vpon þi brest þou schalt go, and erþe þou
schalt ete alle dayes of þi lijf. Vnreste I schal put
35 bitwene þee and þe womman, and þi seed and hir seed ;
sche schal trede þin heed, and þou schalt aspie to hir
hele." § To þe womman forsoþe God seyde : "I schal
multiplie þi dissesis and þi | conseyuynges ; in sorowe   F. 64 b.

18. MS. aud.

þou schalt bere children, and þou schalt be vndir þe
power of þe man, & he schal haue lordschip on þee."
§ To Adam forsoþe he seide : " For þou hast herd þe
vois of þi wijf, and þou hast ete of þe tre of þe which
I comaundide þat þou schuldist not ete, cursid is þe   5
erþe in þi werk ; in traueile þou schalt ete of it alle þe
dayes of þi lijf ; it schal buriowne to þee þornes and
breris, and þou schalt ete þe eerbis of þe erþe ; in þe
swoot of þi face or cheer þou schalt ete þi breed, vnto   10
þe tyme þat þou turne aʒeyn in-to þe erþe of þe which
þou art taken ; for poudir þou art and in-to ₙoudir þou
schalt turne." § And Adam clepide þe name of his wijf
Eue, þoru þat þat sche was modir of alle þingis lyuynge.
For þe Lord God forsoþe made to Adam and to his wijf   15
leþeren cootis and cloþide hem, and seyde : " Se, Adam
is maad as oon of | us, knowynge good and yuel.   Now
panne [lest] perauenture he put out his hond and take
also of þe tre of lijf and ete and lyue eueremoore,—"
And þe Lord God sente hym oute of Paradys of delyte
þat he worche þe erþe of þe which he was taken ; and   20
he þrew out Adam, and he se[t]te cherubyn bifore
Paradys of delyte, and a flawmynge swerd and plyaunt
to þe wey of þe tre of lijf to ben kepte.

F. 65.

**This þat suwiþ now aftir was doon aftir þat Adam
was cast out of Paradys in-to þis woful place.**   25

Aftir þat Adam and Eue weren cast out of Paradys, þei
wenten in-to þe west, and maden hem þere a taber-
nacle, and þere þei dwelten seuene dayes, wepinge, sorowynge, and criynge in grettist tribulacyoun. Aftir þo seuene
dayes þei bigunnen to hungir ; þei souʒten mete and foun-   30
|den noon þat þei myʒten ete. § And þanne seyde Eue to
Adam : " My lord, I hungre soore.   Whi go ʒe not to
seke þing þat we myʒten ete and þereby lyue, if perauenture oure Lord God wole loke on us, and haue mercy
on us, and clepe us aʒein to þe stide þere we woneden   35
first ? " § Thanne aroos Adam aftir þo seuene dayes, and
ʒede aboute in þe lond oþere seuene dayes, and foond

Adam and
Eve are
driven from
Paradise,
and can find
no food.

F. 65 b.

16. *Catch-word* us.   21. MS. sente.

no sich mete as þei hadden in Paradys. § Thanne seyde
Eue to Adam eft: "My lord, I dye for hungur. Wolde
God þat I myȝte dye, or ellis þat I were slayen of þee,
for-whi for me is God wrooþ wiþ þee." And þanne
5 seyde Adam : "Greet is in heuene and in erþe his
wrappe ; wheþir it be for þee or for me, I noot." §And
eft seyde Eue to Adam : "My lord, sle me, þat I may
be doon awey fro þe face of God, & fro þe siȝt of hise
aungels, so þat oure Lord | forȝete to be wrooþ wiþ þee,
10 so þat he myȝte lede þee aȝeyn in-to Paradys ; for-whi
for þe cause of me þou art put out þerof." § Thanne
seyde Adam : " Eue, speke no moore so, leste oure Lord
God sende his malysoun upon us. How myȝte it be þat
I schulde putte myn hond in-to my flesch, þat is to seye,†
15 how myȝte it be þat I schulde sle my fleisch ? But
aryse, go we and seke we where-wiþ to lyue, and ne
stynte we not to seche." § Thanne þei wenten and
souȝten nyne dayes, but þei founden not siche as þei
hadden in Paradys ; napeless siche þei founden as beestis
20 eeten. § Thanne seyde Adam to Eue : " Oure Lord God
delyueride mete to beestis, but to us he deliueride mete
of aungels. But make we sorowe [and doo penaunce]
bifore þe siȝt of oure Lord þat made us fourty day|es, if
happily oure Lord God þat made us forȝeue us and
25 ordeyne us where-wiþ to lyue." § Thanne seyde Eue to
Adam : "My lord, sey me what is penaunce, or how we
schulden do penaunce ; leste happily we taken upon us
þat we may not fulfille, and oure preyers be not herd,
and God turne his face fro us, if we fulfille not þat we
30 han bihote. § Thou, my lord, why seist þou so ? Whi
þouȝtist þou to do penaunce, for I haue brouȝt þee to
tribulacioun ?" § Þanne seyde Adam to Eue : " Myȝtist
þou nott suffre as manye dayes as I may ; suffre as
manye, and þou schalt be saaf. I schal suffre fourty
35 dayes and seuene, for al þing was maad, confermyd, and
blessid in seuene dayes. Arise, and go þou to þe flood
of Tygre, and bere a stoon wiþ þee, and stonde þere-on
in þe watir vp to þe necke, and lete no word come out

F. 66.

F. 66 b.

They do
penance in
Jordan and
Tigris.

14. MS. *repeats* How myȝte it be . . . þat is to seye.
15. soule *crossed out before* fleisch.

of þi mouþ ; for we beɴ | vnworþi for to praye God, for
oure lippis ben vnclene, for we eeten of þe forboden tre.
Be þere fourty dayes, and I schal go in-to þe flum
Iordan, and be þere fourty dayes and seuene, if happily
oure Lord God wole haue mercy of us." § And Eue ȝede   5
in-to þe watir of Tygre, as Adam bad ; & Adam ȝede
in-to the flum Iordan, and leyde his stoon in þe botme
of þe watir, and stood þere-vpon to þe necke in þe flood ;
and þe heer of his heed was spred abrood on þe watir.

Se now þe sorowynge of Adam here.   10

§ Thanne seyde Adam : "I seye to þee, Iordan, gadere
to-gydere þi wawis and alle lyuynge beestis wiþ-inne þee,
and comeþ aboute me and maakiþ sorowe wiþ me. Not
for ȝou-silf make ȝe sorowe, but al for me ; for ȝe han
not synned, but I wickidly aȝeyns my Lord | haue synned. 15
Neiþir ȝe diden ony defaute, neiþir ȝe ben bigylid f[ro]
ȝoure sustenaunce, neiþir f[ro] ȝoure metis ordeyned to
ȝou ; but I am bigylid f[ro] my sustenaunce which was
ordeyned for me."

Se now how alle lyuynge þingis sorowiden to-gydere 20
wiþ Adam.

Whanne Adam hadde maad al þis lamentacionɴ wiþ
sikynge and soruful teeris, þanne alle lyuynge þingis
on erþe, fisch, foul, and beest, cam[eɴ] aboute hym
makynge sorowe wiþ hym, and þe watir also soruyngly 25
stood stille in þat tyme of preiynge. § Thanne Adam
wiþ teeris criede to þe Lord fro day to day, so þat his
vois wexide hors. § And whanne nynetene dayes of
sorowynge weren fulfillid of Adam and of Eue and alle
lyuynge þingis þat sorowiden wiþ hem for her synne, 30
þanne his ad|uersarye þe feend, stirid wiþ wraþþe and
enuye to hemward, transfyguride hym in-to a fayr
ymage, and wente to þe flood of Tygre þere Eue was
sorowynge, and cam to hir and wepte wiþ hir.

Now se how þe feend trecherously spak to Eue.

Satan de-
ceives Eve,
and per-
suades her
to forsake
her penance.

§ Þanne cam þe feend to Eue and seyde : " Come out
of þe flood and wepe no more, for þou art dischargid of
al þin oþir penaunce, for God haþ seen ȝoure sorowis,

5 and haþ forȝeue ȝou ȝoure trespassis at þe preyer of me
and of alle opere aungelys. Þerfore come now out, for
Adam þi lord is out, and God sente me to þee, to lede
Adam and þee to ȝoure sustenaunce aȝeyn which ȝe
hadden in Paradys, and losten for ȝoure synne. And

10 perfore come out, þat ȝe weren at ȝoure mete þat is
maad redy." § Þanne Eue wente out of þe wal|tir, and

F. 68 b.

hir flesch was greene as gras for coold of þe watir, and
whanne sche cam to lond sche fel down for feblenesse,
and lay þere stille as deed almoost a day ; and þe deuel

15 took hir up and cumfortide hir, and brouȝte hir to Adam.
§ And whanne Adam say hir, he cryede weþynge : " O

Adam
denounces
Satan.

Eue, where is þe werk of þi penaunce ; how is it þat
oure enemy haþ þus bigylid þee, þe which bigylide us
fro oure dwellynge place in Paradys and oure goostly

20 ioye ? " § Whanne Eue herde þis, sche knew hir-silf
bigylid þoru þe feend, and fel grouelynge to þe erþe, and
þanne was hir sorowe doublid. § Þanne Adam fel
down, and his sorowe doublide, and cryede and seyde :
" Curside be þou, deuel ; what eylide þee at us ; what

25 haue we doon to þee ; why doost þou sich malice to us ;
haue we ouȝt bynome þee þi | ioye or þi honour ; whi

F. 69.

fiȝtist þou þus aȝeins us, þou envious deuel and
wickid ? "

Se now þe answer of þe deuel to Adam.

Satan relates
how he was
cast out of
Heaven
because he
would not
worship
Adam.

30 Þanne answeride þe deuel sorufully and seyde : " O
Adam, al myn envye, malyce, and sorowe is þoru þee, for
þoru þee I am kepte fro my ioye and cast out of myn
heritage þat I hadde in heuene among aungels, and for
þee I am cast out in-to erþe."

35   Þe answer of Adam to þe deuel.

Adam answeride and seyde to þe deuel : " What haue
I do to þee, or wherfore blamest þou me ? Þou were
vnknowen to me, ne I wiste not of þee."

Now þe answer of þe deuel to Adam.

The deuel seyde to Adam : " Þou woost not what þou
seist, for in þat day þat þou were maad, I was cast down
fro heuene ; and whanne God blew in þee þe spiryt of
lijf, and þou were ma|ad to þe liknesse of God, and   5
Miȝhel ledde þee bifore God, and God seyde : ' Lo, I
haue maad Adam as oon of us,— ' "

Se now how Miȝhel wolde haue Adam to be worschipid by Goddis ordynaunce.

" Miȝhel went forþ and clepide alle aungels, and seyde :   10
' Worschipe ȝee þe ymage of God, as God haþ comaundid.'   And þilk Myȝhel firste honouride him, and
clepide and seyde to me : ' Honoure þe ymage of oure
Lord God.'   And I answeride and seyde : ' Nay, nay ;
I haue not to doone to worschipe Adam.'   § Whanne   15
Miȝhel chargide me to worschipe þee, I seyde to hym :
' Where-wiþ chargist þou me ?   I wole not worschipe a
foulir þan I am.   I am fairer þan he, and I was afore
alle creaturis ; and cer he was, I was maad ; and þerfore
he schal worschipe me, and I not hym.'   And oþere   20
aungels þat herden þis wolden not worschipe hym.

§ Than|ne seyde Myȝhel : ' Worschipe þou þe ymage of
God, or God wole be wrooþ wiþ þee.'   And I seyde to
hym : ' If God be wrooþ wiþ me, I schal sette my seete
on þe sterris of heuene, and be lijk to hym þat is alþir   25
hiȝeste.' "

Se now how Lucifer was putt out of heuene for his pryde and vnobedience.

§ " Thanne God was wrooþ wiþ me, and comaundide
þat I schulde be dryuen out of heuene, and out of my   30
ioye, wiþ myn aungels ; and so by þe cause of þee we
ben cast out of oure dwellynge, and put here in-to erþe.
And anoon I was brouȝt in sorowe and angre, for I was
put out of al my ioye, and þou were put yn alle delycis
and murþis.   And þerfore I bigan to be envyous to   35
þee-ward, and I myȝte not suffre þee to be so in ioye, ne

23. MS. wrooþ *crossed out after* wrooþ.

lyue in so myche murþe. But þanne I wente and bigi-
lide the | womman, and wiþ hir I bigilide þee f[ro] alle   F. 70 b.
þi delicis, murþis, and ioyes, riȝt as I was put out of my
glorious beynge." § Whaɳne Adam herde þis, he criede
5 wepynge, and seyde : "Lord God, my lijf is in þin
hondis ; make þat þis wickid aduersarye be fer from me,
for he sekiþ eueɼe in al þat he may to spille my soule.
Lord, graunte me þe ioye þat he lees !" § Whanne Adam   Adam com-
þis lamentacyoun hadde maad, þe deuel vaneschide   pletes his
                                                         penance.
10 awey fro his siȝt, and Adam truly fulfillide þere fourty
dayes and seuene in penaunce in þe watir of Iordan.

Now se here firþirmoore how Eue spak to Adam.

§ And Eue seyde to Adam : "My Lord God lyueþ ;
to þee is grauntid lijf, and my lijf is grauntid to þee ;
15 for at þe firste tyme, neiþir at þe laste, þou were not
cursid ; but I am cursid and bigilid, for I kepte | not þe   F. 71.
heestis of God.   And now depɑrte me fro þe liȝt of
þis lijf, for I wole be departid fro þe siȝt of þee, for I
am not worþi to se þee, neiþir to haue murþe of þee ne
20 cumfort for my wickidnesse ; but I wole weende as fer
as I may in-to þe west, and dwelle þere til þat I dye."
And sche wente forþ in-to þe west wiþ greet sorowe, and   Eve departs
made hir a wonyinge styde to dwellen ynne, and wepte   into the
                                                             West.
þere-ynne bittirly ; and þat tyme sche hadd go wiþ
25 childe þre moneþis. § And whanne þe tyme cam of
birþe, sche was trauelid wiþ manye dyuerse sijknessis.
And sche mette wiþ oure Lord, and seyde to hym :
"Lord, haue mercy on me and helpe me," and God
herde hir not, neiþeɼ hadde mercy on hir.   § And sche
30 seyde to hir-silf wiþ moornynge ·cheere : "Who schal   F. 71 b.
now do my lord to wyten of my wo ? I preye [ȝou],   Warned of
liȝ|tis in heuene, whaɳne ȝe turnen a-ȝeyn in-to þe eest,   her sickness
                                                           by the lights
þat ȝe schewe my sorowes to Adam myn husbonde." As   of Heaven,
soone as sche hadde þus preyed, hir dissesis weren   Adam visits
                                                           her.
35 openyd to Adam.   § And whanne Adam knew hir
sorowes, he seyde : "Þe dissese of my wijf Eue is comen
to me, and þerfore, leste þe wickid addir þe feend come

2. MS. for.   31. MS. þe.

and fi3te wiþ hir, I wole go and visyten hir." And he
wente forþ, and foond hir in greet sorowe and dissose.
§ And anoon whanne Eue say him, sche seyde: " My
soule and lijf is wel refreyschid þoru þe si3t of Adam."
Þanne seyde Eue to Adam : " Now, good lord, preye   5
for me, þat I my3te be delyuerid fro þese worste peynes."
And Adam preyede to God for hir.

Se now here of þe midwyues of Eue and of þe delyueraunce of Caym hir child.

F. 72.

The birth of Cain.

And þanne þere camen ' twelue aungels | and two   10
vertues, þat is to seye, two opere ordris of aungels,
stondynge al aboute hir, boþe on þe ri3t syde and on þe
lift syde. § And Mi3hel stood on þe ri3t syde and
touchide hir face and hir brest, and he seyde to hir :
" Eue, þou art blessid for Adam, þat is, for the penaunce   15
and þe preyers of hym ; for þoru hise preyers we ben
sent to þee, þat þou my3te vndirstonde help and socour
of Goddis aungels. But ryse þou, and make þee redy to
þe birþe, for þi tyme is ny3." And sche made hir redy
þerto, and sche childide a sone wiþ sorowe. § And   20
anoon þe child roos up and ran forþ and took gras in
hise hondis and 3af to hise modir, and þei clepiden
his name Caym. § Thanne Adam took Eue and hir
child, and ledde hem in-to þe cest. And oure Lord God

F. 72 b.

sente Mi3hel þe archaungel to sowe dyuerse seedis, | and   25
3af hem to Adam, and tau3te Adam to wirke and to tilye
þe lond and to haue fruyt to lyue by, and alle þe
generaciouns aftir hem.

The birth of Abel.

Now anoon suwynge here aftir Adam cumpanyede wiþ his wijf.   30

§ Thanne Eue conseyuede and bare a sone þat hi3te
Abel, and Caym and Abel woneden to-gydere. And

Eve's dream.

Eue seyde to Caym : " My dere sone, as I slepte my-
pou3te I say þe blood of Abel þi broþir falle in þin
hondis." And þe same sche toolde to Adam, and Adam   35
seyde : " I drede þat Caym schal sle Abel ; þerfore þei
schulen be departid and dwellen a-sundir." And þei

maden hem dwellynge placis þat oon fer fro þat opere,
and maden Caym a tylier of erþe, and Abel a scheparde.
And ȝit aftirward Caym slouȝ Abel.

Se how Caym slouȝ Abel.

5 § That tyme þat Caym slouȝ Abel, thanne | Adam was
an hundrid and þritti ȝeer oold. Aftir knew Adam Eue
his wijf, and gate a sone þat hiȝte Seth. Þanne seyde
Adam to Eue : " I haue bigeten a sone for Abel, þe
which Caym slouȝ." § Thanne lyuede Adam aftir he
10 bigat Seeth eiȝte hundrid ȝeer, and bigat þritti sones and
two and þritty douȝtris. Alle hise children weren sixti
and fyue, whiche multiplieden greetly on þe erþe.

F. 73.

The birth of Seth.

§ This þat sueþ telliþ how Caym slouȝ Abel, and of
þe veniaunce þat God took of Caym (Genesis ii[i]jᵒ).

15 AFtir manye dayes, Caym schulde offre of þe fruytis
of þe erþe and ȝiftis to þe Lord ; Abel forsoþe
offride þe firste bigeten of hys flok and of þe fatnesse of
hem. And þe Lord biheld to Abel and to hise ȝiftis ;
to Caym forsoþe and to hise ȝiftis he bihelde not. And
20 Caym was greetly wrooþ, and þere-wiþ fille his cheer.
And þe Lord seyde to hym : " Whi artow wrooþ, and
whi þere-wiþ falliþ þi cheer? Schaltow not resseyue,
if þou doost wel? ellis forsoþe yuel, anoon in þi ȝatis
þi † synne schal be at þee. But vndir þee schal be
25 þe appetyte of him, and þou schalt haue þe lordschip of
him." And Caym seyde to Abel his broþir, " Go we
out," and whanne þei weren in þe feeld, Caym aroos
aȝeins his broþir Abel and slouȝ him. And þe Lord
seyde : " Caym, where is Abel þi broþir?" Which
30 answeride : " I woot nere where ; am I þe keper of my
broþir ? " And he seyde to hym : " What hast þou do?
Þe vois of [þe blood of] þi broþir crieþ to me fro þe
erþe. Now þanne þou schalt be cursid upon þe erþe,
which openede his mouþ, and took þe blood of þi broþir
35 of þin hond. Whanne þou worchist þe erþe he schal
not ȝeue to þee | hyse fruytis ; vagaunt and fer fugytif
þou schalt be on erþe alle þe dayes of þi lijf."

The slaying of Abel.

F. 73 b.

F. 74.

5. *Catch-word* Adam.   24. MS. þi þi synne.

Se þe answer of Caym to his Lord God

§ Thanne Caym seyde to þe Lord God : "Moore is
my wickidnesse þan þat I disserue forȝeuenesse. So,
þou caste me out þis day fro þe face of þe erþe, and fro
þi face I schal be hid, and I schal be vagaunt and fer   5
fugitijf in erþe ; alle þanne þat schal fynde me schal sle
me." And the Lord seyde to hym : " It schal not be
doon so, but al þat schal sle Caym schal be seuenefoold
poneschid." And þe Lord sette a signe in Caym, þat

The gener-
ations of
Cain.
ech þat fyndiþ hym schulde not sle him. § And Caym   10
passide out fro þe face of þe Lord, and dwellide fer
fugitijf in þe erþe at þe eest place of Eden.   Caym
forsoþe knewe his wijf, which conseyuede and bar

F. 74 b.
Ennok ; and he bildide a cytee, and | clepide þe name
of it aftir þe name of his sone Ennok.   § And Ennok   15
gate Irad, and Irad gaat Mauyael, and Mauyael gaate
Matusael, and Matusael gate Lameth, þe which took
two wyues, þe name of þat oon Ada, and þe name of þat
oþere Sella ; and he gaat Iabel, þat was fadir of dwellers
in tentis and of schepardis ; and þe name of his broþir 20
Tubal, he was þe fadir of syngers in harpe and orgon.
Sella gate Tubalcaym, þat was an hamer-smyth and a
smyth into alle werkis of bras and of irun, and þe sistir
of Tubalcaym, Noema.   And Lameth seyde to hise
wyues Ada and Sella : "Heere ȝe my voys, wyues of   25
Lameth, and herkne ȝe my word ; for I slouȝ a man
in-to wounde, a ȝonge wexynge man in-to my wannesse.
Veniaunce schal be ȝouun of Caym seuenefoold, of

F. 75.
Lameth forsoþe | seuentisithe seuenfoold." § Forsoþe ȝit
Adam knew hys wijf, and sche bar a sone and clepide   30
þe name of hym Seeth, seiynge : "God sente to me
anoþir seed for Abel, whom Caym slouȝ."   But and to
Seth is boren a sone, whom he clepide Enos ; þis bigan
inwardly to clepe þe name of þe Lord (Genesis iiijto).

Adam re-
lates to Seth
how he was
rapt into
Paradise.
§ And Adam seyde to Seeth : "Sone, heere me, and   35
I schal telle to þee what I say and herde aftir þat we
weren cast out of Paradys. I and þi modir as we weren
in orisoun, Miȝhel þe archaungel, Goddis messanger, cam
to me, and I say ordris of aungels as þicke as wynd beynge

in a fair cercle, and I say a chare, and þe whelis þerof as fier.
Þanne I was raueschid in-to Paradys, and þere I say
oure Lord, and his semelaunt was as fier breꝝnynge,
and his | cheer was so briȝt þat I miȝte not endure to   F. 75 b.
5 loke þere-upon ; and a greet multitude of aungels weren
a-boute þe beemys of þe briȝtnesse of hys semelaunt.
§ And I say a-noþer wondirful cumpanye of aungels
beynge on his riȝt syde and lift syde ; and I was in greet
dreede, and made my preyer to God in erþe. And my
10 Lord God seyde to me : 'Wyte þou wel þat þou schalt
dye, for þou forȝete my comaundement, and herdist þe
word of þi wijf which I ȝaf to þee to be þin vndirlyng
and þi soget at þi wille, and þou obeyedist to hir and
not to me.' "

15   **Se now here þe preyer of Adam folewinge.**   Adam's
prayer to
God.

§ Thanne seyde Adam : "Now whanne I herde þese
wordis, I fel down to þe erþe and seyde : ' Lord moost
myȝtful and moost merciable, God boþe blessid and
meke, ne forȝete not þe worschipful name of | þi dignyte,   F. 76.
20 but conuerte þou my soule, for I dye, and my spiryt
passiþ out of my mouþ. Ne caste me not a-wey fro þi
face, which þou hast maad of þe sliym of þe erþe ;
neiþir putte þou hym bihynde, þat þou hast norischid
wiþ þi grace. Bihold on me, Lord, how þi wordis
25 brennen me.' "

     Lo now, how God spekiþ to Adam.   God's
answer.

"And oure Lord God seyde : 'For þin herte is sich
þat þou louest science and goodnesse, and repentist þee,
þou schalt not be doon awey fro þi kunnyng, and þe
30 seed þat comeþ of þee, þat wole serue me, schal neuere
be lore.' § And whanne I herde þese wordis, I honouride
hym lowly on þe erþe, and seyde : ' Þou art God with-
oute bigynnyng and eendyng, and e[uery] creature owiþ
to worschipe þee and loue þee. Þou art aboue alle
35 liȝtis s[chy]|nynge, þou art verry liȝt of lijf, þou art sich   F. 76 b.
þat no tunge may telle ne comprehenden in witt. § O

4. not *written above the line.*
33. MS. *faded.*   35. MS. *faded.*

þilk greet vertu of God, alle creaturis ȝeuen to þee
honour and preisinɡ; whanne þou hast maad mankynde
þoru þi greet vertu, it bihoueþ þee to be worschipid.'
§ And anoon as I hadde preyed þis,† Miȝhel þe archaungel of God took myn hond and caste me out of 5
Paradys in þe visitaciouns fro þe siȝt of God. And
Miȝhel helde a ȝerde in his hond, wiþ which he touchide
þe watris þat weren in þe circuyte of Paradys; & wiþ
þe which touching of þe forseid ȝerde þei congyliden
to-gydere in-to yse. And I wente vpon hem, and 10
Miȝhel wente wiþ me, and ladde me aȝeyn in-to þe place
of Paradys fro þe which he raueschide me, and efte

F. 77.

aȝeynward | he ledde me to þe lake þere he raueschide
me."

The
prophecy of
Adam.

Se now how Adam schewide to his sone Seeth þingis 15
þat weren to-comynge aftir.

§ "Now, my sone Seeth, heere me, and I schal schewe
to þee þe pryuytees þat ben to come, and þe sacramentis
þat ben schewid to me; for whi I vndirstood and knewe
þingis þat ben to come in þis world temperal þe whiche 20
God made for mannys kynde, þat is to seye, I hadde
my knòwinge and myn vndirstondyng of þing þat is
to-comynge by þe etynge þat I eet of þe tre of vndirstondynge. § Also I vndirstood þat God schal schewe
him in foorme of fier, and go out of þe seete of his 25
maieste, and he schal ȝeue to men hise heestis, and make
hem holy in the hows of his maieste. And God schal

F 77 b.

sche|we to hem a meruelous place of his magiste, vpon
whiche þei schulen make dwellynge placis in erþe; and
þere þei schulen bigge an hous on erþe to her God. 30
And þei schulen breke hise comaundementis, and her
holy place schal be brent, and her lond schal be forsake,
and ech of hem schal be dryu[en] fro oþir, for þei wolen
wraþþe God. And þe seueþe day God schal make hem
saaf, and brynge hem aȝein to-gydere, and eft þei 35
schulen bigge newe housis to her God, and þanne schal
þe laste hous of God be betir saued þan þe first. And

4. MS. þis þis Miȝhel.   33. MS. dryñe.

eft soone schal schrewidnesse ouercome riȝtwijsnesse,
and eft schal God dwelle with men in erþe to be seyen,
and þanne schal riȝtwijsnesse bigynne for to schyne,
and [en]emyes schulen no moore power haue to [noy]
5 ony man þat trowiþ in God. And he | schal saue his   F. 78.
folk, and þe wickid men schulen be poneschid and
departid from God, for þei wolden not kepe hise heestis
ne his lawe, and God schal reyse a saaf peple to be
maad wiþ-outen eende. And wickide men schulen put
10 Adam out of his kyngdom, and aftirward who þat wole
of þat kyngdom loue heuene and erþe, nyȝtis and dayes,
and alle creaturis worschipynge to þe Lord ; and þei
schulen not breke hise comaundementis, ne þei schulen
not chaunge hise werkis. And men forȝetynge þe
15 comaundementis of God, þei schulen be chaungid ; for
God schal putt out wickide men, and riȝtwise men
schulen dwelle as riȝtwijsnesse in þe siȝt of God. And
in þat tyme men schulen be purifyed of-her synne by
watir of Cristendom, not | willynge to be purified by   F. 78 b.
20 watir. Wijs is þat man þat amendiþ his soule, for whi
þere schal be a greet day of iuggement a-mong synful
men, and her deedis schulen ben enqwerid of riȝtwijs
God her inge."

Se now how Adam clepide to-gydere alle hise children,   Adam calls his children to him.
25   **and enfoormede hem of manye þingis, and**
    schewide hem þat he was nyȝ þe deeþ.

A Nd whanne Adam was of nyne hundrid and pritty
ȝeer oold, he wiste wel þat hise lijf dayes schulden
soone eende. He seyde to Eue : " Gadere to-gydere alle
30 my children bifore me, þat I may speke to hem and
blesse hem eer I dye." And þei camen to-gydere in
þre partyes bifore his preiynge place where Adam hadde
preyed to oure Lord God, and þei camen to-gydere wiþ
o vois, seiynge ; "What sey ȝe to us, fadir ? Whi | ben   F. 79
35 we gaderid hidir, and whi liggist þou in þi bed ? Sey to
us what is þi wille, þat we do it."

        4. MS. *faded*.

Now Adam spak to hise children.

§ Thanne Adam answeride and seyde: "My children, me is ful wo, and wiþ sorowis I am trauelid." And hise children seyden to hym: "Fadir, what is it to haue yuel, and wiþ sorowis to be traueylid?"   5

How Seeth spak to Adam his fadir.

§ Thanne seide Seeth to Adam his fadir: "Lord my fadir, happily þou hast desyrid for to ete of þe fruyt of Paradys, of þe which sumtyme þou eete; and þerfore, I suppose, þou liggist þus in sorowe. Wiltow þat I go   10 and neiȝhe þe ȝatis of Paradys, and do dust on myn heed, and falle doun to þe erþe bifore þe ȝatis of Paradys, and crye in greet lamentacioun, preiynge oure Lord, and

happily he wole heere me and | seende hys aungel to me, to brynge me þat þou desirist?"   15

Now Adam spak to Seeth.

§ Thanne Adam answeride and seyde: "Sone, I desyre no þing, but I waxe ful sijk and haue greet penaunce in my body."

The answer of Seeth to Adam.   20

§ Seeth answeride: "Fadir, I noot what sorowe is; þerfore sey þou what it is and hyle it not."

Se whi Adam was put in Paradys.

§ Thanne seyde Adam: "Heeriþ, alle my children, whanne God made me and ȝoure modir, and putte us   25 in Paradys, and ȝaf us alle þe trees berynge fruyt to eten of whanne we wolden, but oonly of þe tre of knowynge good and yuel, þat stondiþ in þe myddil of Paradys. § Þus God putte us in Paradys, and ȝaf me power in þe eest and in þe partye þat is aȝens þe   30

norþ, and to ȝoure modir he ȝaf fro | þe south vnto þe west, and ȝaf us two aungels to kepe us. Þe tyme cam þat þese aungels wenten in-to þe siȝt of God hym to honoure. Þanne anoon þe feend foond a place in ȝoure modir, and counseilide hir to ete of þe forboden tre;   35 and sche eet, and profride me to ete, and I eet. And

anoon oure Lord God was wrooþ to us, and seyde to me :
'For þou hast forsake my comaundementis, and þat
I ordeynede to þee þou hast not kepte, se, now I
schal caste in-to þi body seuenty woundis of dyuerse
5 sor[o]wes ; fro þe coroun of þin heed vnto þe sole of þi
f[oo]t alle dyuerse membris of þi body be þei turmentid.'
Lo, manye sijknessis God haþ ordeyned us, and to alle
oure osprynge." § This Adam seiynge to hise sones,
he is taken wiþ greet sorowis, and he cr[i]ede wiþ greet
10 vois and seyde : " Wh[at] | schal I, wrecche, do þat am
putt in þese sorowes ? "

F. 80 b.

Se now þe lamentacyoun of Eue.

Adam sends
Eve and
Seth to
Paradise to
ask for the
oil of life.

And whanne Eue hadde herd þis sorowe of hir husbonde, sche bigan to wepe and seyde : "Lord God,
15 putte þ[ese] sorowes in me, for whi I haue trespassid,
and nott he." And sche seyde to Adam : "Good syre,
ȝeue me part of ȝoure sorowes, for my defautis maken
þee to haue sorowes." § And Adam seyde to Eue :
"Arise and go wiþ þi sone Seeth, and neiȝhe ȝe to þe
20 ȝatis of Paradys, and caste erþe on ȝoure heedis and
falliþ doun and makiþ sorowe in þe siȝt of oure Lord God,
if happily he wole haue mercy on us, and happily he
wole comaunde an aungel to go to þe tre of mercy, fro
þe which renneþ oyle of lijf, and happily he schal ȝeue
25 ȝou of þat medicyn, þat ȝe may þere-wiþ a-noynte me,
þat I myȝte be lissid of þese sorowis, in þe whiche I
brenne and am ful wery of."

F. 81.

Se now how Seeth and Eue his modir wenten toward Paradys.

On the way,
a serpent
bites Seth in
the face

30 § Thanne Seeth and Eue his modir wenten towarde
Paradys in haaste. And while þei ȝeden by þe weye,
sodeynly þere cam an addir, a foule beeste wiþ-outen
pytee as it were a feend, and boot Seeth wickidly in þe
face. And whanne Eue say þat, sche bigan to wepe
35 bittirly and seyde : § "Allas is me, wrecche, for I am
cursid, and alle þat kepen not þe comaundement of God."

5, 9, 10. MS. *faded*. 6. MS. **feet**.
15. MS. þi. 26. *Catch-word* te.

And sche seyde to þe addre wiþ a greet vois : "O þou
cursid beest, whi doutist þou nott to hirte and to a-noye
Goddis ymage, and how artow hardy to fiȝte wiþ it, or
þi tooþ to greeue so worþi a creature ?" And þe addir

F. 81 b.

answeride and sey|de wiþ a greet voys : "O þou Eue, 5
wheþir oure schrewidnesse be not a-fore God, ne hap
not God stirid oure woodnesse aȝeins ȝou ? Sey, þou
Eue, how were þou so hardy to ete of þe tre which oure
Lord God comaundide þee to ete not of ? For bifore
hadde we no power in ȝou, but aftir þat ȝe hadde broke 10
Goddis bidding we hadden power in ȝou."

Se now how Seeth spak to þe serpent.

§ Thanne seyde Seeth to þat cursid worm : "Cursid
be þou of God ! Go awey fro þe siȝt of men, close þi
mouþ and waxe þou dombe, cursid enemy and distrier 15
of riȝtwijsnesse ; go fro þe siȝt of Goddis ymage til God
calle þee aȝeyn to be prouyd what þou art. § And þe
worm seyde to Seth : "I may not wiþstonde þi
biddyng, but now I go awey fro þe ymage of God."

F. 82.

| § Seeth and Eue hys modir wenten to þe gatis of 20
Paradys, and þei tooken þe dust of þe erþe and casten
on hir heedis and on her facis, and þei fillen grouelynge
to þe erþe and maden greet sorowe,† preyinge God to
haue mercy on Adam, and þat he wolde sende an aungel
to brynge hem of þe oyle of þe tre of mercy to hele wiþ 25
Adam.

St. Michael
prophesies
of the com-
ing of Chris-
tianity.

Seeþ þe answer of þe aungel to Seeth.

§ The aungel Mychael appeeride to hem and seyde : "I
am [þe] archaungel Mychael, þat am ordeyned of God
keper of mannys body. I sey to þee, Seeth, wepe no 30
moore, preiynge for þe oyle of mercy to anoynte wiþ
þe body of thi fadir Adam, for þou myȝte not haue of
þat oyle of mercy til fyue þousinde ȝeer, two hundrid,
and eiȝte and twenti be eendid."

23. MS. sorowe and preyinge.
27. *First* þe *above the line.*   29. MS. an.

Se here þe profecye of Cristis co|mynge.

§ "Thanne schal come on erþe Ihesu Crist, Goddis
sone, and schal be baptisid in þe flum Iordan, and he
schal dye and rise aȝeyin and go to helle and anoynte
5 þere Adam þi fadir and brynge him [to blisse] and alle
feiþful deede men wiþ hym, whiche anoyntynge schal
dure wiþ-outen eende. § Thanne schal Crist Ihesu stye
up, and he wole lede þi fadir in-to Paradys to his tre
of mercy. And go þou now to þi fadir and sey to
10 hym, þe tyme of hise lijf-dayes ben doon, for aftir
sixe dayes his lijf schal passe, and þanne þou schalt see
grete wondris in heuene and in erþe among þe briȝt
aungels of heuene." § Whanne Miȝhel þe archaungel
hadde seid þis, anoon he vaneschide awey. § And Eue
15 and Seeth turneden aȝeyn hoomward, and tooken wiþ
hem swete oynementis | (odoramenta†), þat is, Nardum
and Crocum and Calamynte and Cynamonium and Canel.
§ And whanne þei camen hoom to Adam, þei teelden
how þe serpent hadde byten Seeth his sone.

20 ## Se now how Adam spak to Eue.

§ And Adam seyde to his wijf: "Biholde what þou
hast do to us. Þou hast brouȝt to us a greet dissese, and
synne to al oure kynde. But soþly al þis þat þou hast
do to us, and alle þingis þat ben doon, schewe to oure
25 children aftir my deeþ, þat þei þat schulen come of us
here-aftir ne shulen not ben wrooþ to bere þe dissesis
þat þei schulen haue, ne þe sorowis; þanne þei schulen
curse towardis us, and seye : § 'These dissesis han oure
former fadir and modir brouȝt us to, þat weren in þe
30 bigynnyng afore us.'" § Whanne Eue herde þis, sche
bygan to | wepe and make doel. § And, as Miȝhel seyde
bifore, aftir sixe dayes Adam diede, and eer he diede, he
seyde to hise children : "Biholde ȝe now on me, my
children, and seeþ now how I dye, and þe noumbre of my
35 dayes in þis world ben nyne hundrid ȝeer and thritty.
§ Whanne I am deed, birieþ me aȝens Goddis ȝerd in þe

16. MS. ordoramenta.
25. MS. to *expunged, and* of *added above the line.*

feeld of his dwellynge place." And whanne he hadde
seyd þis word, he ȝeeldide up þe spirit, and þe sunne
waxide derk, and þe moone and þe sterris eiȝte dayes
lastynge.

Eve and her
children
mourn for
him.

Se now how Seeth and Eue his modir diden aboute 5 Adam.

§ And whanne Seeth and Eue his modir hadden
leyd forþ the deed body of Adam, þanne þei kneliden
a-down oon tyme and saten anoþir tyme, and þei greetly
sorowiden upon þat deed body, and euere þei lokiden 10

F. 81.

| downward towardis þe erþe, clappynge her hondis vpon
heedis, and þei puttiden down her heedis to her knees
soore wepynge, and alle her children also.

He is buried
by the angels
in Paradise.

Se now how Myȝhel þe archaungel spak to Seeth.

§ And þanne Miȝhel þe archaungel spak to Seeth 15
and to Eue his modir as þei weren stondynge at Adams
heed.   And he seyde to Seeth : " Aryse up fro þe body
of thi fadir, and come to me that þou may se þi fadir,
and þe ordynaunce þe which oure Lord God purposide
to do wiþ hym, for he haþ mercy on hym at þis tyme." 20
Th[an]ne alle aungels trumpiden vp, seyinge : " Blessid
be [þou], God, of þi makynge, for þou art now merciable
on hym." § Thanne s[ay] Seeth þe hond of God holden
up and [hel]de hys fadir soule, and took it to Sey[nt]

F. 84 b.

Mychael, and seyde : " Lete þis soule be [in] | thy 25
kepynge yn turmentis in-to þe laste day of dispensacyoun,
and þanne schal I delyuere hym of hise sorowis.   For
soþe, þanne he schal sitte on his ioyful trone, þat
haþ cast hym so lowe."   And ȝit seyde God aȝeyn to
Michael : " Brynge to me þre cloþis of sendel and 30
bismos, and ley oon ouer Adam, anoþir ouer Eue, and
anoþir ouer her sone Abel."   And alle þe ordris of
aungels wenten bifore Adam, and blessiden þe sleep╋ of
þe last eende of hys deeth.

21. MS. faded.   23. MS. faded.   24. MS. faded.
25. MS. faded.   33. MS. adds of þe sleep, crossed through.

Se now here where and how Adam was biryed, and who weren at hys bir[i]yng.

§ And archaungels biryeden þe body of Adam on þe body of his sone Abel in Paradys. § Seeth and [hi]s
5 modir sayen þat the aungels dide, and they merveyliden greetly. Thanne seyden the aungels to hem : | " As ȝee han seen these bodyes biryed, yn the same maner birieþ ȝoure dede bodyes aftirward." § Thanne sixe dayes aftir that Adam was deed,—

F. 85.

10   See now how Eue spak to alle hir childr[en].

†Eue knew that deeth was comynge towardis hir faste. Sche gaderyde to-gydere alle hir sones and douȝtris, and seyde : " Heeriþ me, my sones & douȝtris, what I schal telle to ȝou. Aftir the tyme that ȝoure fadir and I
15 hadden passid Goddis comaundementis, Mychael the archaungel seyde þu[s] to us : ' For ȝoure synne God wole d[istrie] ȝoure kynde, firste by watir, aftirward by fier ; and yn these tweyne alle man[n]ys kynde ben [ponyschid] of God.' "

Eve tells
her children
of the two
judgments
to come.

20 Seeþ now here how Eue techith Seeth to make tablis of stoon.

§ " Therfore heere þou, my sone | Seeth : make þou tweyne tablys, of stoon and of schynynge cley erthe, and wryte there-ynne þe lijf of ȝoure fadir and of me, and tho
25 þingis that ȝee han herd and seen of us. For whanne God schal iuge al oure kynde by watir, the tablys of erthe wolen loose, and the tablis of stoon wolen dwelle ; forsoþe, whanne God wole iuge mankynde by fier, thanne wole [the tablis of stoon loose, and] the tablis of erthe
30 endure." § And whanne Eue hadde seid this to hir children, sche spredde hir hondis a-brood and lokide vpward to heuene, knelynge on the erthe, and preiede to God. And while sche preyede, hir spiryt passide, and

F. 85 b.

Eve orders
Seth to write
the story of
Adam and
her on tables
of stone and
clay.

Death of
Eve.

4. MS. *faded.*   10. MS. childꝼe.
11. MS. see now how Eue. 16. MS. *faded.*
17. MS. *faded.*   18. MS. *faded.*

WHEATLEY MS.   H

þanne alle hir children wepten bittirly, and so with greet moornynge biryeden hir. § And while þei maden sorowe for her modir [f]oure dayes lastynge, Mychael the | archaungel of God appeeride to hem & seyde :

**Se now here how Michael the archaungel techiþ Seth   5
how he schulde moorne and how longe.**

§ " Man of God, make þou noon sorowe for the deeth of thy fadir and of thi modir no lengir than sixe dayes, ne for noon þat dyen ; for the seueneþe day ys tooken of oure vprysynge and reste to come of this world, and 10 in the seueneþe day he took reste of alle hyse werkys."

**Seeþ now how Seeth makiþ þe two tablis bifore
comaundid to hym.**

§ Thanne Seeth made tweyne tablys of stoon and of erthe, and wroot there-ynne the lijf of hys fadir and of 15 hys modir ; and whanne tho weren maad, he leyde hem yn his fadris oratorye, where hys fadir was wont or vsyd to | worschipen almyȝty God ynne. § And aftir Noe flood tho tablis weren founden and seen of manye oon, but þei weren not red. § Aftirward by longe processe of 20 tyme cam Salamon the wiys kyng, and say these tablis and the wrytynge þere-ynne, and he preyede to God that he myȝte vndirstonde the wrytynge of tho tablis.

§ Thanne appeeride to hym the aungel of God, seyinge : " I am þe aungel that helde the hond of Seth whanne 25 he wroot this wiþ an irun, haldynge it in his riȝt hond. And yn these two tablis weren wryten manye wondirful profecyes ; and I sey to thee, Salamon, thow schalt knowe þe scripture þat is wryten in these tablis. And þese tablis weren in þe place where Adam and Eue 30 weren wonyd to preye God, | therfore it bihoueþ thee to make there a dwellynge place to God." § And þanne Salamon clepide these lettris on þese tablis Achiliacos, that is to seye, wiþ-outen techyng of lyppis wryten wiþ þe fyngir of the riȝt hond of Seeth, the aungel of God 35 holdynge it. § Thanne made Salamon an hous in the

3. MS. *faded.*

name of God, men to preyen ynne; and in tho tablis
was founden wryten þat þat was profecyed of Adam
seuene sythis. § And Ennok also profecyede of Noe
flood, and of þe comynge of oure· Lord Ihesú Crist.

The prophecy of Enoch.

5 " Lo," he seyde, " oure Lord schal come in hys holy
kny3thood to make iuggement of men, and to dis[c]ryen
alle the wickide men of her werkis, and of alle the
spekyngis of hem with synners. Wickide men and
gruch|chers, thei seken for to speke aftir her owne

F. 87 b.

10 coueitynge; thei entriden and spaken proudly." § This
is the book of þe generacyoun of Adam.† In the day
in which God made man of nou3t, to the ymage and the
liknesse of God he made hem, male and female he made
hem of nou3t, and he blesside hem, and he callide the

15 name of hem Adam in the day in the which they weren
maad of nou3t. § Adam forsothe lyuede an hundrid 3eer
and þritty, and he gate a sone to the ymage and his
liknes, and callide the name of hym Seeth. § And the
dayes of Adam ben maad aftir that he gate Seth ei3te

20 hundrid 3eer, and he gate sones and dou3tris; and al the
tyme in which Adam lyuede ys maad nyne hundrid | 3eer

F. 88.

and þritty (Genesis v^{to}). And alle the sones of Adam
weren þre and þritti, and dou3tris two and þritty; and
so alle hise children weren þre score and fyue. Blessid

25 be oure Lord God.

AMEN.

Thus eendith thys blessid tretys of oure Fadir Adam.

6. MS. distryen.   11. MS. *repeats* Adam.
23. in *crossed out after* weren.

XIV.

[A PRAYER AT THE ELEVATION.]

**Here bigynneþ a deuoute preyer and an excellent,
that schulde distynctly ben seyd and with greet
deuocyoun betwene þe Leuacioun of þe Blessid
Sacrament and the thridde Agnus Dei.**

Eyl, Ihesu Crist, Word of þe Fadir, Sone of þe   5
Virgyn, Lomb of God, Heelþe of this world, sacrid

Oost, Welle of pytee, | Word and Flesch boren of þe
Virgyn Modir, haue mercy of us. § Heil, Ihesu Crist,
Kyng of aungels, Ioye of seyntis, þe Siȝt of pees, hool
Godheed, verry Man, Flour and Fruyt of þe Virgyn 10
Modir, haue mercy of us. § Heyl, Ihesu Crist, Schyner
of þe Fadir, Prince of pees, ȝate of heuene, Br[ee]d of
lijf, Vessel of clennesse, Child of the Virgyne Modir,
haue mercy of us. § Heyl, Ihesu Crist, Liȝt of heuen,
Prijs of this World, oure hool Ioye, Breed of aungels, 15
Gladnesse of herte, Kyng and Spouse of þe Virgyne
Modir, haue mercy of us. § Heyl, Ihesu Crist, Weye
of swetnesse, Trist of soothnesse, oure hyȝeste Meede,
oure verry Loue, Welle of trewe loue, oure Pees, oure
Reste, and oure eendelees Lijf, borun of the Virgyne 20
Modir, haue mercy of us.

AMEN.

12. MS. brid.

NOTES

I. An Orison on the Passion.

34. "And the nails of wrought iron."

43. [b]ent : so all the Oxford MSS.

52. MS. Bodley 850 reads : "Myn harde hert till it be soft;" similarly the other two. This is probably the original reading; a later scribe did not understand the construction.

55–6. MS. Bodley 850 reads :

> "When þou loked on þⁱ modir fre
> The tyme þou hing vpon þᵉ rode-tre,"

and omits 57–62. This evidently represents the original version, the poem being a meditation exclusively on the sufferings of our Lord. These six lines, which interfere with the division of the poem into 4-line stanzas, are consequently an interpolation.

98. The two lines following this in the MS (see footnote) are clearly a variant on 99–100. They are found in the Oxford MSS., the second line reading, "Be it foule," etc., and the *Meditations* (see Preface, p. vii), ll. 1683–4, with the reading, "Be it serwe to hure and foul to se."

129. **thow**: the Oxford MSS. read " I," but cp. John xiv. 23, et mansionem apud eum faciemus.

134. **hym** : this is strictly tautological, but is found in the Oxford MSS.

II. Hymn to the Blessed Virgin.

4. **emprice of helle** : "Queen of Heaven and Empress of Hell" is a common medieval title of the Blessed Virgin, especially frequent in Lydgate. The origin may perhaps be found in the epithet of *lucifera* applied to her by the Fathers; cp. Cyril, *Homiliae Diversae*, xi. (Migne, vol. 77, p. 1034), Maria Deipara, Virgo mater, Lucifera . . . per quam prodiit lux vera; Ephraim Syrius, *De Sanctissimae D.G.V.M. Laudibus* (ed. Asseman, vol. iii., p. 535), lucifera virgo. Cp Lydgate, *Minor Poems* (ed. MacCracken, E.E.T.S., E.S. CVII., p. 323):

> "O blessed lady ! qweene of þe heghe heven
> Whome clerkes calle þemperyse of helle."

12. **haue[s]**, MS. haueth. This error presumably arose when the 3s. *pr. ind.* endings were altered from *-es* to *-eth* by an East Midland scribe. Probably "hath," 9, " saith," 15, 19 below, are also to be so explained.

54. **[ʒe]** : MS. the. A scribe has apparently wrongly expanded the " þ " here and in 55, 56, 58. Cp. " þyng" for "ʒyng," 139.

70. **wrye** : probably the original form was "wreghe," rhyming with "heghé " in the preceding line.

90. Psalm xxxviii. 3.

91-2. Cp. Godric's *Song to the Virgin:*

> "Sainte Marie, Cristes bur,
> Maidenes clenhad, moderes flur."

99. "But those things which proceed out of the mouth come forth from the heart; and they defile the man," Matt. xv. 18.

103. Unless the line is corrupt "amendes" = "to amendes."

127. Matt. vii. 19.

157-62. Deut. xxii. 1-3.

169. The first of the Five Joys.

183. Cp. Psalm vii. 15, et peperit iniquitatem.

265-8. Mark xii. 42-44; Luke xxi. 1-4.

287. **iustice of lyueraunce**: a justice sent under commission of gaol delivery to try prisoners awaiting the assizes.

297. 1 John iii. 17.

309-10. Matt. xii. 50; Mark iii. 35; Luke viii. 21. Cp. Wright, *Reliquiae Antiquae*, II., 227, "Thou my suster and my moder, and thy sone ys my broder;" *Quia Amore Langueo*, MS. Harl. 1706, F. 10 *b.*: "Thy syster ys a quene, thy brother ys a kyng."

312. **[mys]fare**: the two words beginning with *my* caused scribal confusion.

314. *i.e.* as a base-born brother. The compound "luf-barne," an illegitimate child, is not found in N.E.D.; but cp. E.D.D.

III. Hymn to St. John the Baptist.

3. **fader**: the original word may well have been "sire," as the poet's intention was probably to make the lines alliterate in pairs. Cp. note on 63.

8. **with myrthe schul mete**, *i.e.* shall experience joy. Et multi in nativitate ejus gaudebunt, Luke i. 14.

15. **in wone**, in the dwelling-place, an expletive, signifying "in the world." Cp. alliterative *Alexander Fragment* (E.E.T.S. 1.), 598, "Of any wight*es* in wonne wysest i-holde."

24. **at**: either the Northern form of "to," or a scribal error caused by the "at" in the line above.

32. **þat men were in stede**, with which men were beset. Cp. *Towneley Plays*, xix. 259, "stersman to theym that ar sted in stormes."

44. **me[ns]keful**: cp. *Towneley Plays*, xxix. 388-9, A, marie so mylde . . . Was neu*er* madyn so menskfull here apon molde.

45. **þat [maste] is**: MS. þat is ful. Cp. *St. John the Evangelist*, I., "Of 1. mankynde þat he made, þat maste es of myghte," and II. 172 above: "When thow conceyued God of myghtes maste."

49. Cp. *Cursor Mundi*, 11062-4:

> "Maria . . . was hir-self þe first wom*m*an
> þat lifted fra þe erth iohan."

The incident is found in Petrus Comestor's *Historia Scholastica* and in the *Golden Legend.*

53. **[vn]-borne**: the similarity between *v* and *b* in many MSS. would help to account for this error.

63. **þei bothe**: one would expect "þi sire."

64. þat bright: *i.e.* Christ. Cp. Luke i. 17.

81. Cp. Luke i. 63 (Purveyite version) : And he axynge a poyntil.

89–90. Hawes . . . rotes of þe ryse . . . borion-and bere : all these represent different interpretations of the Vulgate locusta. **Hawes** = oats, though the first example cited in N.E.D. (see "Haw," 4) is of the year 1601. The common medieval form is haver, O.N. hafre. Pliny, in Book xxii., ch. 79 of the *Natural History*, remarks that the seeds of oats resemble small locusts in appearance, and "locusta" is a botanical term for the spiked inflorescence of grasses. Hence, just as the fruit of the carob tree was called "locust" from its appearance, and taken to be the food of the Baptist, it was evidently thought that he lived on oats and barley. That "locusta" was a root is stated in the *Ormulum*, 1. 3213, "Hiss mete wilde rotes," also in *Trinity College Homilies*, E.E.T.S., 53, p. 139, "Moren *and* wilde uni was his mete." Caxton, in the *Golden Legend*, F. clxxxviij., though he knows that locust was flesh of some sort, says, "Somme saye that there ben rootes so callyd." *Cursor Mundi* agrees with our text, "And liued wit rotes and wit gress," l. 11109.

[hente] : this restores the alliteration ; "toke" was caught by the scribe from the line above.

104. As fel on þe twelft day, *i.e.* Christ manifested Himself, as at the Epiphany.

[þe tille] : these words have been transferred to the beginning of the next line, and changed to "vn-to þe."

105. to þe : the same mistake occurs in the Towneley *Deliverance of Souls*, where St. John the Baptist says :

> "The holy gost from heuen discende
> As a white dowfe downe on me than ;
> The fader voyce, oure myrthes to amende,
> Was made to me lyke as a man."   ll. 69–72.

It may have arisen from a misunderstanding of Mark i. 10. In the parallel *York Play*, l. 70 has " hym."

131–4. This comes from the opening of the story of the Baptist in the *Golden Legend*, ch. 86 : "Johannes baptista multipliciter nominatur. Dicitur enim propheta, amicus sponsi, lucerna, angelus, vox, Helias, baptista salvatoris," etc.

132. þat worthy wight, *i.e.* Christ.

IV. The Seven Penitential Psalms.

1–8. This prologue is taken from D, where it is headed :

"Here bigynneþ þe prologe of þe seuene salmys in englysche by Richard Hampole heremyte."

R substitutes for l. 8 :

> "By frere Richarde Maydenstoon,"

and adds the verse :

> "In Mary ordre of þe Carme,
> þat bachilere is in dyuynite ;
> Sheo bar Jesu in wombe & barme,
> þat moder is and mayden fre.
> To þat childe þen in hir arme,
> Whiche for vs henge on rode tre,
> þat he for wreche do vs no harme,
> Hym to queme þese salmes saye we."

It is not probable that these verses belonged to the original. The words, " to make oure mone," should be compared with the phrase, apparently peculiar to this poem, " to make mones," 20, 109. It is also improbable that the author should divide his name and description between two verses. The original poem probably had no prologue ; the first form of the prologue was that of D, a later innovator changed the last line and added another verse. Ll. 1–8 are printed here in order to make the numbering of the lines the same as that in Adler and Kaluza's text.

9. Psalm vi. ; against Anger.

11–16. K, W, differ from all other MSS. here. Presumably the MS. from which they are derived had lost the opening verse.

20. **to make mones** : so also Ad, H, Ad_2, L, D_2, Do. D, Ful greet mater of mournyng monys, so A, R, Ro. Cp. 109. N.E.D. does not record any M.E. use of "mone" in the plural.

21. **cast in creke** : so K, Ad, R, A ; D, L, read "dyke"; D_2 has "greet "; Do, "But whanne my body y^s badde & weke." The word appears to be identical with "cratch" in N.E.D. and E.D.D., a rack, hurdle or bier, but the derivation from Germanic *crippja is not easy to reconcile with the present form. Except for the wealthy, coffins were not commonly used for burials until about the seventeenth century, the body being wrapped only in a winding-sheet (see J. E. Vaux, *Church Folk Lore*, 1902). In Brand's *Popular Antiquities of Great Britain*, 1905, Vol. I., p. 250, there is an illustration of such a burial from a Breviary in the British Museum. Brampton, however, has "whan I am lokyn in leed," v. 47.

85. **[be]**. So all MSS. but K, which has "flesch ynamed."

89. Psalm xxxii., Vulgate xxxi. ; against Pride.

99. The MS. reading seems to have arisen from a confusion between "the gode lord" of A, H, Ad_2, and "oure lord god" of R, Ro.

104. The original reading may be D_2, "to wroþerele werk in litul whyle," corrupted in A to "God wyll be wroth ryȝht in a whyle."

109. **to make mones** : cp. 20. So Ad, H, Ad_2, D_2, Do, but D, R, A, Ro, mater of greuous gronys.

116–17. Cp. A, With thornes priked. All other MSS. have present tense here. Cp. *Dives and Pauper*, 1496, v. iiij. col. 2 : "The mytre on his [*i. e.* the bishop's] hede betokeneth þᵗ crowne of thornes þᵗ cryste bare on his hede for mannes sake. And therfore the mytre hath two sharpe hornes in token of ij sharpe thornes" (quoted in Manning, *The People's Faith in the Time of Wyclif*, p. 14).

118. **pyne** : the other MSS. read "peyne" ; cp. 181.

123. R, A, Ro read :

> "þourȝe shrifte wol I from me þrowen
> Alle my misdede," etc.

This evidently represents the original version. Cp. Ad :

> "In scrhifte schal y ben aknowe
> Of my misdede."

132. **Forg[a]f** : Vulgate, remisisti. Ad, forȝaf. All other MSS. have imperative sg. here.

155–6. The scribe has omitted these two lines, misled by the similar endings

of 154, 156. The original ending of 156 was probably, as in D₂, "wiþinne &
oute."

193–4. Cp. Brampton, **xxx.** :

> "In herte thei may be merye and glad,
> That ryȝtfully here lyif lede."

197. **sight** : D₂ has "suyte," R, "sute," probably the original reading.
[c]ladde : so Ad, H, R, L, D₂.

201. Psalm xxxviii., Vulgate xxxvii. ; against Gluttony.

217. Cp. Brampton, xxxiii., In my flesch I have non hele.

218. **w[re]th[l]i** : so Ad, A ; H, wroþely ; D₂, Do, worþeli.

235. **[fir]st** : so all MSS. except K.

249. **fayry** : so R, H, D₂, Do ; Ad₂, faire ; A, freylty; Ad, hurtynges; D, L,
disseiȝtes.

259. **fadres** : so K ; Ro, fader ; all other MSS., frendes.

[for]warde : so all MSS. but K.

266. Cp. Brampton, xxxix., My sorwe I may noȝt fro the hyde.

285. **[N]ow** : so Ad₂ only.

289–96. The scribe has omitted this verse, misled by the fact that both it
and the following verse begin with *Et qui.*

303–4. "Then shall the Truth unveil Himself, (showing) how sin," etc.
Perhaps the nearest to the original is Ad₂ :

> þan wil þe sothe it-self vnswathe,
> And shewe þᵗ envy hath many slayn.

Cp. Ad, And schewe þourȝw wham þe soule ys sclayn.

305. **no-[þing]** : so D, R, A, L ; D₂, nowȝt y hurd.

310. **gyl[e]**, MS. gylt. This reading is also found in Ad, but the metre
requires a dissyllable.

314. **opynnyng** : perhaps a corruption of "upmenynge" in K ; cp. D₂,
vpnemyng ; Vulgate, redarguciones. This word is omitted in the MS., although
there is plenty of room for it in the line.

331. **stere** : so D, translating Vulgate commoventur.

339. **gode** : K, H, Ro read "not"; Ad, good, D₂, god.

341. **[out]** : so R, A, Ad, H, Ro, Do.

342. **þat to deeth were** : K, "that the to dethe," and so all others, except
Ad₂, which has a different verse, and L, which reads, "On olyue mount whan it
was niȝt."

361–8. Cp. Brampton's *Penitential Psalms*, v. 51 :

> Now I am ful lytel bounde
> To manye, that were to me beholde ;
> Whan I am deed, and leyd in grounde
> Here love is waxen wonder colde.
> They bakbyte me manye folde ;
> Evyll for good thei quyten me :
> I am aferd thei be to bolde
> Of ' Ne reminiscaris, Domine ! '

With the first four lines of this verse, compare stanza 36.

385. Psalm li., Vulgate l. ; against Lust.

397. **strengh[e]** : K, strynge ; A, Ad₃, D₂, Do, sterynge ; D, Ad₁, strengþe;
R, Ad₂, Ro, fondyng.

419. K, Thi wordis asketh ; so Do. This approaches nearer to the Vulgate.

422. [thi] f[eit]h : MS. my flesch ; K, Ad, D₂, thi feyth ; Do, þy fey. Cp. Numbers xv. 31, "Because he hath despised the word of the Lord . . . that soul shall be utterly cut off."

437. This line is also omitted in Ro. Here the scribe has added an eighth line : I pray to þe bothe day & nyght. In both cases he has been misled by the similarity of "knytte" and "knyght"; there is no near relation between the MSS.

448. is : so Ad, H, D, D₂, Ad₃ ; K, Ro, V, R, A, L, Do, has. For the construction, see Kellner, *Historical Outlines of English Syntax*, p. 76.

503. [thow] : so R, Ad₃ ; MS. vs ; K, V, Ad, H, the; L, ȝow (probably for þou) ; Ro omits the pronoun, and D has a different line. The syntax evidently puzzled scribes. D₂, keeping the reading of W, changes 504 to "To wasshe vs from þis worldly welthe."

522. [a]greuyd : so A, Ad ; Do, y-gryuyd.

529–36. Rev. xxi., and Eph. ii. 19–22.

532. This is not stated in Revelation, but was a commonplace of medieval theology ; see Richard Rolle, *Libri Psalmorum Enarratio*, and St. Remigius, *Enarrationum in Psalmos Dauid Liber*.

533–4. The walls are made up of the members of the Church ; these lines are therefore probably a corruption of D :

T[w]o (MS. tho) testamentis acordeþ in (MS. into) oon ;
The wallis were togidere brouȝt, etc.

544. the fendes fere : so K, Ad, Ad₂, Ad₃ ; D₂, Do, þe feendes fier ; R, H, Ro, helle fyre ; V, helle fere ; A, cursyd fere. Possibly "helle" was altered to "fendes" by a scribe or scribes who did not recognize "fere" as the Kentish form of "fyre."

545. Psalm cii., Vulgate ci. ; against Covetousness.

550. There [nedith] noon : so all other MSS.

565. frely : cp. A, thorow freylty ; Ad₂, þurgh freelness ; cp. also *Cursor Mundi* 25689, Man . . . þat frelli fra þi frenscep fell. For the spelling, cp. "holy," III. 58.

571–2. "Similiter cremium est lardum adustum : a quo scilicet omnis pinguedo recessit. Corpus ergo christi in cruce fuit . . . sicut cremium : quia sanguine suo preciosissimo fuit euacuatum" (*Sermones dormi secure*, fol. xlii., 1523, attributed to Richard Maydenstoon). I have not found this in the Commentaries of St. Augustine, Richard Rolle, St. Remigius, or Peter Lombard. The sermon is said to be "collectus ex libro Jacobi de Voragine," but I have not found it in the *Golden Legend*.

587. The scribe omitted this line, being misled by the two consecutive lines beginning with the same three words.

589. The metre requires "theues," as in R, Ad, Ro, H, (?) þe uyse, or "Jues," as in A. Probably "theues" was the original word, altered to "theef" under the influence of Luke xxiii. 39.

593–4. The story of how the pelican slays its young, and, after mourning over them for three days, revives them with its own blood, is found in St. Augustine (*Migne*, Tom. 36, 37, p. 1299) and in Peter Lombard (*Glossa psalterii Dauid*, 1478), under this verse. Trevisa, *Bartholomeus Anglicus*, 1582, p. 186, says that the young birds are bitten by the serpent ; similarly, *Dives et*

Pauper, Tenthe Precepte, ciii. St. Augustine doubts the truth of the legend, and explains the allusion as referring to the Virgin Birth of Christ: "Solus enim sic, ideo solitudo : in solitudine natus, quia solus ita natus."

597–600. Cp. St. Augustine : "Post nativitatem ventum est ad passionem : a quibus crucifigebatur? numquid ab stantibus? numquid a lugentibus? Ergo tanquam in nocte ignorantiae ipsorum, et tanquam in parietinis ruinae ipsorum. Ecce nycticorax et in parietinis, amat et noctem. Nam nisi amaret, unde diceret, *Pater, ignosce illis, quia nesciunt quid faciunt* (Luc. xxiii. 34)?" In Ad₂ we have a different idea :

> " And as þe nyght crowe dwell can
> In an rewayn place or in an heth,
> So all þe tyme here þat Crist was man,
> Ful fewe men hym knewe vnnethe."

602. As "so" has no equivalent in the Latin, it probably arises from a scribe's repetition of the first two letters of "solitarye." D₂, Do, read "resteth solitari."

603–4. The reference is to Psalm lxxxiv. 3, " Yea, the sparrow hath found an house, and the swallow a nest for herself, where she may lay her young." Cp. St. Augustine, p. 1068 : "Dixerat exsultasse cor suum, et carnem suam, et his duobus reddidit passerem et turturem, cor tanquam passer, caro tanquam turtur. . . . Turturi autem dedit et pullos, id est carni."

608. MS. hadde Ie ; so D₂.

626. wiþ vprisyng : "through my being raised up on the Cross." Other texts read "upliftyng." The commentaries do not take this verse as referring to Christ, but to man exalted by being made in God's image, and cast down in his fall.

659–60. Cp. Rev. xxi. 14. According to St. Augustine, the stones of Sion were the prophets. So Peter Lombard : Lapides sunt prophete ; ibi premissa est predicatio inde sumptum est euangelicum officium. Serui ergo i.e. apostoli agnoscunt in lapidibus, i.e. in prophetis, eloquia dei. So also St. Remigius : apostolis tuis intelligibiles erant prophetae.

665. The scribe has omitted two verses, continuing from the Latin of this stanza to the English of stanza 86.

681, etc. The rhymes in K are : seeth, beeth (*pl.*), fleeth (?*pl.*), stef (= stiff), which show its southern type. The present version is corrupt in that it has no pause after 684. Cp. D :

> At him, þat alle vices fleye,
> Crist Jesu, etc.,

and K, Of hem, etc. ; Do, H, of hym.

693. flyten : the rhymes point to a short vowel. The reading of K is therefore probably correct : How he was for us, etc. ; all MSS. agree with this.

702. [a] : K, D₂ also omit this, but all other MSS. have it.

736. feri[þ] : so D₂ ; Ad, feride.

737. [halfundele] : the difficult word caused trouble ; cp. Do, þe myddyl del ; L, Calle me not in half dayes of hele.

739–40. " For they pass as imperceptibly as the sun crosses the meridian, or the clouds move in the sky." Ro gives a different version :

> For of tyme or it be mydday melle
> þai glidyn als þe clowdes clere ;

i. e. many are cut off in middle life. D, L, substitute, "Mi dayes ben schort, þi dayes ben fele."

767. **schalt þou** : K reads "schal hit"; but Ad, "þou schalt ben."

776. **[þat]** : so D, R, A, Ad, Ro, L.

777. Psalm cxxx., Vulgate cxxix. ; against Envy.

816. **sale** : so L; all other MSS. read "dale" here; probably a reference to the valley of bones, Ezek. xxxvii.

828. **boþe lyme and lith** : so also K, evidently a corruption of Ad, lyet euery lith ; H, lyþe euery lyʒtht. The reference is to the Real Presence, cp. *Prayers at the Elevation*, E.E.T.S., 98, pp. 24, 25. In MS. Harl. 3810, Pt. 1, pp. 10*b*–13, there is a Miracle of the Blessed Sacrament, in which the refrain of each stanza is :

> "God is very God in forme of brede."

The meaning is brought out at the expense of metre and rhyme by D_2 : In forme of breed þat on þe autere lith ; and Do, in auter þat lyth.

839. R, A read, And we schul up to heuene & helle ; this is an emendation of "heuene helle" found in D_2, and as "heuene hylle" in Ad and H. This adds another to the examples of Kentish rhymes.

841. Psalm cxliii., Vulgate cxlii. ; against Sloth.

907. **[h]orowe** : so D, R, H.

915–6. **soone** has been transplanted from 915 to 916 by scribal error.

919. **blende** : the original reading was, I think, "pende," as in R, a Kentish form of O.E. pyndan, to enclose, confine, dam up (of water). The readings of Do, peynes pende ; H, paþ pynde ; D_2, peys schende ; and finally D, soulis schende, show the difficulty this word gave

929. **[Lord]** : so D, L, R, A, Ad, H, D_2, Do.

936. MS. of ; so Ad, D_2.

941. This is corrupt. Except K, all MSS. read "þogh" for "þat" and "now" for "not" (D_2, al).

943. **[ʒit]** : so Ad, H, Ro, D_2, Do.

Ro has an additional verse :

> Gloria patri & filio & sp*irit*ui sanc*t*o.
>
> To þe fadyr, sone, & holy gost
> Be ioy & blys wi*th*outen hende,
> þa*t* o god es of myghtes most ;
> He fende vs fro þe fals fende,
> Kepe vs fro com*b*urance i*n* euere coste,
> þa*t* syn no senschyp vs noght schende,
> And g*ra*unte vs g*ra*ce we be not loste,
> Owte of þis warld wen we sal wende.
>
> Amen : amen : p*ar* charite : amen.

V. Lessons from the Dirige.

59/12. **wi*th*-stonde** : Vulgate subsistam ; Purvey, abide ; Hereford, stonde still ; Cp. *Lessons of the Dirige*, 32, "I ne may withstonde þe y-wisse."

60/3. **to my soule** : so Hereford ; Vulgate, in amaritudine animae meae ; *Lessons*, 35, To my soul y wole speke in bitternesse.

60/4. **Wil þou not** : Vulgate, noli.

60/11. **[wite] þou for**: so Add. 27592 and Hereford; a literal translation of Vulgate, et scias quia; Purvey, wite that.

60/26. **fleischis**: Vulgate, carnibus; Purvey and Add. 27592, fleisch.

61/5. **[þi my3t]**: so Purvey; Vulgate, potentiam tuam.

61/8. **in stockis**: Vulgate, in nervo; Purvey, in a stoc, but the sg. form is very rare, only one other example being noted in N.E.D. The word presented difficulties; cp. *Pety Job*, 265, In a synew thow hast my feet sette; *Lessons*, 153, In synne þou settest my fot *and* hede.

61/23. **and þou leetist þee worþi**: Vulgate, et dignum ducis; Purvey, and gessist thou it worthi.

61/28. **at þee**: Vulgate, apud te.

þat mown not passe: Vulgate, qui praeteriri non poterunt; Purvey, whiche moun not be passid.

61/30. **of a marchaunt**: Vulgate, mercenarii; Hereford, of an hirid man; *Lessons*, 204, of harde man.

62/8. **goostly liknesse**: Vulgate, immutatio, (?) v.r. imitatio; *Lessons*, 234, Tyl my folwyng come to myn insi3t; Purvey, chaungyng.

62/12. **aftir my deede**: secundum actum.

62/29. **I seyde to rotennesse . . . þou art my sistir**: Vulgate, Putredini dixi: Pater meus es; mater mea, et soror mea, vermibus. *Lessons*, 267–70, I sayde to stynke *and* rotenesse, "My fader *and* moder arrt 3e;" and to wormes y sayde þysse: "My systren *and* my brethern both be 3e."

62/31. **Where is þanne myn abidynge and my pacience? þou art, Lord my God.** The office here differs from the Vulgate text; cp. v. 44, *Pety Job*.

63/7. **My mouth**: Vulgate, os meum. The same mistake is made in *Pety Job*, 529–30:

> To my skyn my mouth ys, lo,
> And cleued fast, as ye se may.

þe fleisch wastid: this represents the ablative absolute; Purvey, whanne fleischis weren wastid.

63/27. **led[d]ist**: Vulgate, eduxisti.

64/2. **[o]rrour**: so Hereford; MS. errour, so MS. Add. 27592; Purvey, hidousnesse; Vulgate, horror.

64/4. **fro þe erþe**: et terra; *Lessons*, 333, from erþe breþe.

64/10. **Whanne þou . . . fier**: *Sarum Manual*, Quando caeli movendi sunt et terra; so *Prymer*, p. 69.

64/11. **What schal I þanne, moost wrecche, what schal I seye**: quid ergo miserrimus quid dicam.

64/16. **wil þou not**: noli.

64/18. The *Sarum Breviary* here repeats the Responsory, Libera me, etc. (64/3).

64/19. **Brennynge soulis**, etc. This and the following Versicle form the special commemoration for All Souls' Day. After the Repetition, "Whanne þou," etc., the *Sarum Breviary* repeats the Responsory, Libera me, etc.

64/21. **þere we go**: This should read, "Whanne þou schalt come," etc. *Sarum Breviary*, quantae sunt tenebrae! Dum veneris. So in *Lessons*, 370, Allas in þysternesse we go; MS. B.M. Add. 36683, an English Primer closely following Purvey's text, omits these words.

64/31. **in peynes**: in poenis tenebrarum.

criynge and seiynge . . . aȝeynbier : this should be the Versicle.
64/32. **Delyuere me, Lord, of þe weyes of helle.** *Sarum Breviary* has here :
Qui portas.

VI. A SONG OF MERCY AND JUDGMENT.

9. Cp. Add. 31042, Who so euer es þer in moste sure.
19. **siche as [þe]e seeme :** such beings as beseem thee. The line as written
in the MS. is found in Add., but not in Lambeth, which evades it by a non-
rhyming line, " þi passioun make us briȝt & schene."
27–8. The MS. being written as prose, " man," first displaced within the
line, was easily transferred to the next one.
37. **of al þing :** especially.
57–8. Hebrews xiii. 5. This had probably been included among the Words
from the Cross in some "Complaint " poem. Cp. the *Northern Passion*, 1755–60,
where Matt. viii. 20 is so reckoned, also *Cursor Mundi* 24284–6 (*The Sorrows
of Mary*) :

> For wite þou well, i am wit þe
> Wit-vten tuin, and sua sal be
> Fra nu for euer mare.

VII. A PRAYER FOR MERCY.

12. **[for] :** so Cb. MS.
28–48. Cb. MS. substitutes :

> Mercy for þy comaundement
> That I haue ofte-tymes y-broke,
> And in þy seruyse be neclygent
> And mony a wylde word haue spooke.
> What were to þe to ben a-wrooke
> On hym þat may noþer fyȝt ne flee ?
> Lette neuer thyn Eris fro me be loke,
> But euer, good Iesu, haue merci on me.

50. **[do] :** so Cb. MS.
52. Cb. MS. But part with me al of þy grace.
54. **Th[er] :** Cb. MS. as.
55. Cb. MS. In Heuene þer to haue a place.

VIII. GOD'S COMPLAINT.

3. MS. enteynt. Following on this, Bodley 596 reads " entent."
4. Cp. *Reproaches :* Popule meus quid feci tibi, aut in quo contristavi te ?
responde mihi. MS. Adv. probably gives the correct reading :

> "Myne awne pepill, quhat have I wroucht
> To the, that is to me so faynt ?"

15. **boþe quike & greene :** *i.e.* both the animal and the vegetable world. Cp.
Genesis i. 29, 30.
17–18. *Reproaches :* Quia eduxi te de terra Aegypti : parasti crucem Salvatori
tuo . . . Ego eduxi te de Aegypto, demerso Pharaone in mare rubrum, et tu
me tradidisti principibus Sacerdotum. Ego ante te aperui mare, et tu aperuisti
lancea latus meum.
25–28. *Reproaches :* Quia eduxi te per desertum quadraginta annis, et manna

cibavi te, et introduxi te in terram satis bonam, parasti crucem Salvatori tuo . . .
Ego te pavi manna per desertum, et tu me caedisti alapis et flagellis.

33. **ledde**: Douce 78 reads "To by thy soule my lyfe y bedde," so also
Rawl. C. 86. Though these are both late MSS., they seem to give the best line.

36. MS. Adv. inserts a verse here :

> "My wyneyhard I plauntit the,
> Full of gude saver and swetnes
> And nobil seid of all degre;
> Bettir in erd nevir sawin wes.
> Quhy suld thou thus-gat fra me fle,
> And turne all in-to bittirnes ?
> The croce, for my reward, to me
> Thou grathit and gaif,—this is no leis.
> Yhit had I evir to the grete hers,
> Resistand thame that to the rynd,
> And puttand the of mony a pres;
> Quhy arttow to thi freind unkynd ?"

Cp. *Reproaches:* Ego quidem plantavi te vineam speciosissimam, et tu
facta es mihi nimis amara, aceto namque sitim meam potasti, et lancea per-
forasti latus Salvatori tuo. . . . Ego te exaltavi magna virtute, et tu me
suspendisti in patibulo crucis. After this point there is no more connection
with the *Reproaches.*

38. **Fre wille**: so Harl., Bodley, Douce, Rawl., Adv. ; the two Lambeth MSS.
read "ful riche," but the next two lines point to ours as the correct reading.

56. **foreyne**: so Bodley; Lambeth 853 reads, "As he that synne neuere dide
steyne;" Lambeth 306, feyne; Adv., As sum with syn that nevir did nane. The
allusion seems to be to the Parable of the Prodigal Son, and the rare word
"foreyne" is therefore the original reading. It is not elsewhere recorded
in this signification.

57. **How dide Marye Maudeleyne** : *i.e.* she turned from a life of sin, and
came to Christ. Lambeth 853, however, reads, "what y dide to."

58. **And what [I] seyde to Thomas of Ynde** : John xiv. 6, I am the way, the
truth, and the life : no man cometh unto the Father, but by me.

77. **aȝeyn**: the reading of the Lambeth MSS., "also," would improve the
metre.

87. "With cursing sufficient to cry out for vengeance, thou wilt assay," etc.

XII. Hymn from the Speculum Christiani.

2. **m[ayden]**: so Add. 37781, Roy. 17 A. xxvii. ; Rawl. liturg. g. 2, mayde,
Vernon, Modur and Mayden mylde : Marie, þenk on me !

5. **Ma[rye]** : so Ashmole, Royal, Lambeth. Cp. Vernon, Marie Mylde, þat
Modur art : And mayden hol and clene.

8. **oute of dette** : *i.e.* out of sin. The Lambeth scribe has emended to "fro
wicked dethe."

10–14. These lines in the *Speculum* are as follows :

> Gete me grace in thys lyue
> To knowe and kepe ouer all thyng
> Cristen feith and Goddes byddyng
> And trewly wynne alle that I nede
> To me & myn clothe and fede.

19-20. In the other MSS. these lines are placed before ll. 17–18.

26. In the other MSS. this line is, "Helpe me lady with alle thy might."

32. In the other MSS. this line is, "That thei mow here so do."

35. [And]: so Lambeth, Add. 37787; Royal, Rawl. liturg. omit.

35–8, 43–4 : the *Speculum* MSS. omit these lines.

46. A better reading is given in Dr. Patterson's text: shrift and housling.

50. After this point the *Speculum* MSS. add 10 lines, omitting 51–2.

52. So Royal.

XIII. LIFE OF ADAM AND EVE.

76/7–9. **whanne oure Lord . . . of hem** : cp. Genesis ii. 1, a summary of Genesis i. 1–25, given in full in H$_2$ and D.

76/8. [and erþe]: so all MSS. except D$_2$.

76/9–28. **God say . . . weren ful gode** : Genesis i. 26–31, Purvey's revision.

76/28–31. **The Lord God . . . soule ȝeuynge lijf**: Genesis ii. 7, Hereford's version.

76/31–78/6. **Adam was maad . . . alle Goddis children** : cp. MS. Harl. 526, ff. 76–77.

76/34. **of foure corners of the world** : the reason is given by Rabbi Eliezer: "If a man should come from the east to the west, or from the west to the east, and his time comes to depart from the world, then the earth shall not say, 'the dust of thy body is not mine, return to the place whence thou wast created'" (ed. Friedländer, 1916, p. 77).

77/9. **of foure maner of wyndis he was enspirid** : Cp. *Secrets of Enoch*, xxx. 8, his spirit from my breath and from the wind.

77/14. **Annocolun** : Latin MS. Anathalim, from Gk. ἀνατολή.

77/17. **Dysis** : Latin MS. stellam miridianam nomine Dysis, Gk. δύω, to set. This should of course be the west, as it is in the Vernon text and in Jean d'Outremeuse.

77/19. **Arthos** : Latin MS. Arthos, Gk. ἄρκτος.

77/21. **Mensembryon** : Latin MS. Mencembrion, Gk. μεσημβρινός, southern. Again, naturally, the Vernon text and Jean d'Outremeuse are correct.

77/27. [Adam]: "fiet" has been added in the margin, but there was not room for "Adam." The error, therefore, appears here for the first time. The same mistake is found in A, which is thus almost certainly descended from our text. See also Notes on 92/10, 96/8, 16, 31. The Latin verse does not appear in any of the Latin MSS. of the *Vita* in the British Museum. MS. Harl. 956, however, which gives the account of the making and naming of Adam followed by Jean d'Outremeuse, has the following :

> Anathole, disis, arthon, mesembrion, omnes
> Quatuor hee partes esse feruntur Adam.
> Anathole dedit A, disis D; contulit arthon
> A, mesembrion M ; collige, fiet Adam.

The last two lines (with "et" in mistake for "A") are found in Harl. 3362, preceded by a four-line Latin rendering of "When Adam delved and Eve span."

77/31. **couetous** : Latin vagus, apparently confused with "avarus."

77/32. **stoonys of þe erþe** : Latin adds : vnde sunt ossa eius.

77/33. **bittir** : Latin auarus, evidently written or read as "amarus."

78/5. **þese holy profetis and alle Goddis children** : Latin episcopi & sacerdotes

& omnes *sancti* et electi. E, H_3, L, D read "goddes chosen," H, D_2 simply "goodis." Hence there was probably an illegible word in the English MS. from which both H and this text descend, of which one scribe was able to read the first two letters. A also reads "children," and adds, "The 9 *parte* is of fier wher-of he is angrit and moved to wratht."

78/6–11. **Forsoþe þe Lord . . . good and yuel:** Genesis ii. 8–9, Hereford's version.

78/10. **Paradys:** MS. adds, "and took man and put hym in paradys," which has been caught up by a scribe from the following line. H tries to rationalize it by adding "and he plantid the tree," etc.

78/11–80/23. **Thanne þe Lord . . . to ben kepte:** Genesis ii. 15–iii. 24, Hereford's version. The description of the four rivers, ii. 10–14, is omitted, probably because they have already been enumerated.

78/22–4. **Al þing forsoþe . . . name of hem;** Hereford, "al thing forsothe of soule lyuynge that Adam clepid, that is the name of it. And Adam clepide alle thingis hauynge soule, and al volatile of heuene, and alle beestis of the erthe, bi her names."

78/27. **fillid:** Hereford, fulfillide; Purvey, fillide; Vulgate, replevit.

78/32. **mannys deede:** man's act, a translation of Vulgate virago. Cp. 'Apostles Dedes," Wycliffite versions.

78/37. **lyuers:** Vulgate, animantibus. L emends to "liberdis."

79/13. **[and eet]:** scribal omission due to the many short clauses beginning with "and." The words are found in all the other MSS.

79/18. **[in]:** MS. and, so also E, H, L, D, D_2; Hereford, at; Vulgate, ad; H_3, yn. A scribe may easily have confused "in" and "&."

79/34. **Vnreste:** other MSS., enemytees; Vulgate, inimicitias.

80/17. **[lest]:** supplied from Hereford; Vulgate, ne forte. Petrus Comestor in his *Historia Scholastica, Liber Genesis,* Cap. xxiv., quotes this as an example of aposiopesis. H, L, D_2 have further disguised it by making the verbs indicative.

80/21. **se[t]te:** so the other MSS.; MS. sente.

80/23. **to þe wey of þe tre of lijf to ben kepte:** so Hereford and H_3, E, L, D; H and D_2 read, "to kepe the weie towardes the tree of liue," following Purvey.

80/26. **þei wenten in-to þe west:** this is not in the printed *Vita,* but appears in all the Latin MSS. of it in the British Museum. In the Greek *Apocalypse of Moses* (Charles, *Apocrypha and Pseudepigrapha of the O. T.,* II. 138), they go into the east, as is presumed by this version, 85/32, 86/24. In the *Book of Adam and Eve,* translated by Malan from the Ethiopic, 1882, a Christian work of the 5th or 6th century, God sent them out towards the west, "because on that side the earth is very broad." They could not go out towards the east, because the Garden itself was on the border of the world eastward, beyond which there was nothing but water encompassing the world and reaching to heaven. God would not send them out towards the north, because on that side there was a sea of water, in which the righteous should be washed from their sins at the last day, and if they washed in this they would be cleansed from their sin and forget it; nor would He send them out towards the south, where the north wind would bring them the smell of the trees of the garden, for in that delight they would forget their transgression.

81/6. **wraþþe:** so all the English prose versions, but the Latin MSS. read

WHEATLEY MS. I

"creatura" (the passage does not appear in the printed *Vita*). Cp. C, 70, His creat*ure* is gret. Evidently "creatura" is corrupted from "creata ira."

81/22. [and doo penaunce]: so H, E, L, D, D₂; H₃, A, omit.

81/32–4. My3tist þou nott . . . schalt be saaf: *Vita*, non potes tantum facere quantum ego, sed tantum fac ut salveris. So H, E, H₃, D, D₂, following a MS. with "et" in place of "ut." B follows a MS. with the reading of Harl. 526, Numq*u*id potes in tantos dies facere & no*n* facis. Dico tibi tantos fac vt volueris.

82/16, 17, 18. f[ro]: MS. for (three times), the same error occurs the first two times in H₃.

83/30. This version of the Fall of the Angels is that of the *Koran*, Chs. 7, 15, 17, 18, 38.

84/8. Here the rubric breaks into a sentence.

84/24–6. I schal sette . . . is alþir hi3este: Isaiah xiv. 13–14. Cp. *Cleanness*:

> "I schal telde vp my trone i*n* þe tramou*n*tayne
> & by lyke to þat lorde þat þe lyft made," ll. 211–12.

85/13. My Lord God . . . grauntid lijf: Harl. 526, Viuit dominus deus meus, tibi concessa Vita. H, my Lorde god leueth to the grace and is graunted to the liffe; this shows a scribal attempt at emendation consequent on the corruption of "lyueth" into "leueth."

85/27. And sche mette wiþ oure Lord: this picturesque detail is found in all MSS. of this version, but is not in the British Museum Latin MSS.

86/20. wiþ sorowe: Latin MSS. et erat lugidus, *Vita* et erat lucidus, referring, of course, to Cain, and to the legend which made him the son of Satan. See *Palestinian Targum*, Genesis iv. 1, and *Pirkê de Rabbi Eliezer*, ed. Friedländer, p. 150.

86/23. Caym: a play upon the similarity of the name to the Hebrew word for a reed, Kânëh (Wells in Charles's *Apocrypha*, etc.).

86/32. And Eue seyde to Caym: in the *Vita* and in B, C, she tells the dream to Adam only.

86/34. in þin hondis: Latin MSS. add: et ore suo deglutivit. This is found in B and C, but not here or in the other prose MSS. There are many variants in the earlier MSS., see Meyer. The passage seems to be founded on a misreading of Genesis iv. 11.

87/6. an hundrid and þritti 3eer oold: H, H₂, L, D add, "For s[o]th Abelle was slaine of Cayme in the yeeris of his age an hundrid and twoo yere."

87/6–9. Aftir knew Adam . . . which Caym slou3: Genesis iv. 25.

87/9. Thanne lyuede Adam . . . and þritty dou3tris: Cp. Genesis v. 4. Petrus Comestor (*Historia Scholastica*, ch. xxix.) says: "Legitur Adam triginta habuisse filios, et totidem filias praeter Cain et Abel;" similarily *Cursor Mundi*, 1215–18. The numbers in the text are founded on the legend that, except in the case of Cain, Eve always bore twins, male and female. See Introduction, p. xxix, and 99/22.

87/15–88/34. Aftir manye dayes . . . of þe Lord: Genesis iv. 3–26, Hereford's version. The result of this interpolation is that the story of the birth of Seth is told twice, almost in the same words (87/6–9, 88/29–32).

87/23. ellis forsoþe yuel: but if indeed (thou dost) evil.

87/36. vagaunt: H, but be vacaunt. Consequent on the error of "vacaunt" "vagaunt" (Vulgate, vagus), a scribe has inserted "but be."

88/27. ʒonge wexynge: so Purvey ; the earlier version reads "litle waxen"; H, litille wexinge, so H_2, H_3, E, L, D.

88/34. inwardly: so Hereford ; H emends to "in worde"; "inwardly to clepe" translates the Vulgate "invocare."

88/35. And Adam seyde to Seeth: both Latin and English texts of Adam's vision are very confused.

88/39. and I say ordris . . . as fier: *Vita*, et vidi currum tamquam ventum et rotae illius erant igneae; Harl. 526, & vidi choros tanquam ventos & rota illius erat ignea. The English version seems to comprise both these, "fair" being originally "fiery." B, who is a careful translator, and uses a different MS., omits the chariot.

89/2. Paradys: in paradiso iusticie, *i. e.* the Paradise of the just ; B, rightwisse paradys. This is the highest of the seven heavens, in which is the dwelling of God, and where the just can hear the voice of God. See Weber, *Jüdische Theologie auf Grund des Talmud und verwandter Schriften*, Leipzig, 1897, 162.

89/20. conuerte: so H_3; other MSS. "comforte"; *Vita*, converte.

90/3. it bihoueþ þee to be worschipid: this is not found elsewhere. It seems to be a repetition of "e[uery] creature owiþ to worschipe þee," above.

90/5. out of Paradys . . . siʒt of God: *Vita*, de paradiso visitationis et iussionis (v.r. visionis) dei. Harl. 526 reads : in medio p., etc., hence B, in to the mydel of p. But the reference is to the heavenly Paradise, separated from the world by waters.

90/11. in-to þe place of Paradys: so the Latin MSS. ; but *Vita*, in locum. Adam was outside Paradise when Michael ravished him into the Paradise of Justice.

90/13. to þe lake: this seems to have arisen from confusion in the Latin source between "locum" and "lacum," which has led to the repetition of the whole sentence. It does not appear in B.

90/28. vpon whiche þei schulen make dwellynge placis in erþe: an anticipation of the following sentence, not found in Latin or B.

91/9-12. And wickide men . . . to þe Lord: *Vita*, et impii punientur a deo rege suo qui noluerint amare legem illius. celum et terra noctes et dies et omnes creaturae obedient ei. This has become in Harl. 256 : et impii ponent Adam regno suo et qui noluerunt amare regni illius celum et terram, etc. The correct version appears out of place three lines earlier, "and þe wickid," etc. This points to its having been a marginal correction, which has been taken by a copyist as an addition. It does not appear in B.

91/17. as riʒtwijsnesse: Harl. 526, sicut iusticia ; it is not necessary to add "askith" from H, which must be a scribal addition, and appears in no other MS. except L and D_2.

91/18-20. men schulen be purifyed . . . purified by watir: *Vita*, purificabuntur homines per aquam a peccatis. condempnati erunt nolentes purificari per aquam. "Condempnati" has in some way become "of Cristendom." The MSS. read "consequenti" or "consequentes."

91/32. And þei camen to-gydere in þre partyes: cp. *Apocalypse of Moses*, v. 3, And all assembled, for the earth was divided into three parts.

92/10. I suppose: these words, which are exceedingly difficult to read in the MS., are only found here and in A.

92/18-19. greet penaunce : cp. B, gret sorwes and desese. Probably l. 21 should read "penaunce."

93/6. f[oo]t : so H.

93/15. þ[ese] : MS. þi ; B, his ; other MSS. þese.

94/28-95/9. Interpolated from the *Gospel of Nicodemus*, ch. xix. ; cp. Meyer, p. 204. The differences are very great, and the version of the prophecy found in B is much nearer the Latin, which reads : Tunc veniet super terram amantissimus Christus filius dei resuscitare corpus Adae, et cum eo resuscitare corpora mortuorum. Et ipse filius dei veniens baptizabitur in flumine Jordanis et, dum egressus fuerit de aqua Jordanis, tunc de oleo misericordiae suae perunguet omnes credentes in se ; et erit oleum misericordiae in generationem et generationem eis qui renascendi sunt ex aqua et spiritu sancto in vitam aeternam. Tunc descendens in terris amantissimus filius dei Christus introducet patrem tuum Adam in paradisum ad arborem misericordiae.

95/5. [to blisse] : cp. C, 793-4, "He shal fordon þe fendis myȝt And leden þy fader to blesse briȝt ;" *Gospel of Nicodemus*, 1275-6, And be baptist in þe flome To brynge þi fadres bale to blysse (E.E.T.S., Extra Series, C., p. 103) ; and *Story of the Holy Rood*, 211-12 (E.E.T.S., 46, p. 68), "And till all þat will sese of sin Sal he gif blis þat neuer sal blin," in each case after the mention of the oil of mercy. Cp. also *Chester Plays*, XVII., 193 (The Descent into Hell), "To blis[se] now I will you bringe." The sentence is probably misplaced, and therefore left unfinished and undeleted by a scribe.

95/16. odoramenta : so L, D, A ; MS. ordoramenta, so B, H₂, H₃ ; H, D₂, adoramenta.

95/17. Canel : originally a gloss on "Cynamonium"; as is "swete oynementis" on "odoramenta." Neither of these appear in B.

In the *Apocalypse of Moses* these spices were taken from Paradise by Adam after the Fall, that he might have wherewith to make offering to God.

95/36. aȝens Goddis ȝerd : *Vita*, contra ortum dei (v.r. diei). "Ortum" has been read as "hortum."

96/8. þanne þei kneliden a-down oon tyme and saten anoþir tyme : this is peculiar to this MS. and A. It does not appear in the Latin, but the reading of H₂, H₃, D, which preserve the following "and," suggests that it has been omitted from these texts.

96/16. as þei weren stondynge at Adams heed : the first three words are a scribal addition which destroys the sense ; *Vita*, et ecce Michahel angelus apparuit stans ad caput Adae. They are only found in this MS. and A.

96/21-3. Blessid be [þou], God, . . . merciable on hym : *Vita*, benedictus es, domine, quia misertus es plasmae tuae.

96/23. Thanne s[ay] Seeth . . . hys fadir soule : *Vita*, tunc vidit Seth manum domini extensam tenentem Adam.

96/28. þat haþ cast hym so lowe : *i.e.* Satan. *Vita*, qui eum supplantavit. Cp. Au. 563-5 :

"& afterward þan schal he
Sitten in þilke selue se
þat Liȝtbern sat, min angel briȝt,"

also C. 889-90 :

"þanne shal he sitten wiþ herte glad
In his trone þat him made,"

which seems to come from a read·ng "plasmavit."

96/30. **þre cloþis of sendel and bismos:** Harl. 526, tres pannos de sindone bissinos. "Bismos" is not recorded in N.E.D., the ordinary form being "biis," from O.F. bysse, as in V. The word is omitted in H, D_2, and may well be due to a mis-reading of the Latin adjective as "bissmos."

96/31. **anoþir ouer Eue:** only found in this MS. and A, and apparently due to the scribe's unwillingness to waste a cloth. In V there are only two cloths. The *Vita* reads: afferte mihi tres sindones bissinas et expandite super Adam. et alias sindones super Abel filium eius. Harl. 526 turns this into: vnum super corpus Ade & alium super corpus filij eius Abel.

In the *Book of Adam and Eve*, Bk. I., ch. lxxix., when Cain had murdered Abel, the earth would not receive his body, but threw it up again three times, the first time because he was not of the first creation, the second time because he was righteous and good, and was killed without a cause, the third time that there might remain before his brother a witness against him. So in the *Apocalypse of Moses*, the first reason only being assigned (§ 40). See Au. 569–73; *Cursor Mundi*, 1075–84.

96/33. **of þe last eende of hys deeth:** *Vita*, dormitatio mortuorum. The reading of H, L, D, D_2, H_3, of his last eende of his dethe, suggests that the three last words are a gloss on the first expression.

97/3. **on þe body of his sone:** so B, A. Harl. 526 reads: & corpus filij eius Abel. A scribe has written "super" for "et," catching the word from a few lines above. H, H_2, H_3, L, D, D_2 read: in the vale of Ebronne as the maister of stories tellith.

97/10. The rubric here breaks into a sentence.

97/11. **Eue:** MS. se now how Eue; this scribal repetition shows that this is not the first MS. to insert the rubrications.

97/17. **firste by watir, aftirward by fier:** so the *Vita*, but in this case there would be no need for tables of earth. The most reasonable account is in Jean d'Outremeuse: sains Mychiel ly avoit dit que Dieu feroit II jugement, dont ly uns sieroit par aighe et ly aultre par feu; mains nuls ne savoit liqueis sieroit devant. In C the judgment is to be by water *or* by fire.

97/18. **ben [ponyschid]:** H, H_2, H_3, L, D, D_2, A, have the same omission.

97/28–30. **thanne wole [the tablis of stoon loose, and] the tablis of erthe endure:** H_2, H_3, L, D, have the same omission. H, D_2 read: than wille the tablis of stone abide and endure; A, then will those tables enduer. B is correct; the passage is a good test of accuracy for a medieval scribe.

98/14–99/10. **Thanne Seeth made . . . and spaken proudly:** this passage is only found in MSS. of Class II. of the *Vita*.

98/14–99/3. This passage differs so greatly from B, as regards language, that it must have been a fresh translation. The prophecy of Enoch is, however, exactly the same.

98/33. **Achiliacos, that is to seye, wiþ-outen techyng of lyppis.** On this passage Meyer gives the following note: "Achiliacas. ἀνυλιακάs = ἀχειροποιήτουs." The word is first found in the Paris MS. 5327, of the eighth or ninth century, where the passage runs: "achylicas quod est in latino inlabicas hoc est sine labore doctrina scriptas," and next in MS. Clm. 17151, of the thirteenth or early fourteenth century, as, "achilicas quod est latine lapideas id est sine labiis doctrina scripta." The whole passage, though not a part of the original *Vita*, is evidently translated from the Greek, and the original Greek word was probably ἀνυλικὰs, *i. e.* not made of matter, of heavenly origin. Corrupted to "achylicas," it was then Latinised as "inlabicas," from the Greek χεῖλος, a lip ; this coined Latin word was afterwards glossed, rightly or wrongly, by various scribes, and also itself either corrupted, or, as in our text, omitted entirely. Of the two MSS. quoted above, the first is wrongly glossed, and the second has the wrong Latin word, taken by the scribe from the description of the making of the tables above. In the fourteenth and fifteenth centuries the confusion grew worse. Meyer quotes "sillabicas hoc est sine librorum doctrina scriptas" (MS. Clm. 5865), and Harl. 495 reads : "aqu*a*illicitas q*uod* e*st* latine inlapidatas i*d* e*st* s*i*ne labiis doct*r*ina scriptas." It should be noticed that the Auchinleck MS., which is based on a very early form of the *Vita*, omits all mention of the angel's having assisted Seth, and consequently of the letters. From the account in 98/14–16 we may conclude that this represents the first form of the story.

99/2–4. þat þat was profecyed . . . Ih*e*su Crist : *Vita*, quod prophetavit septimus ab Adam Enoch dicens ante diluvium de adventu Christi. Cp. Jude 14–16; Enoch i. 9.

99/10–22. This is the book . . . ȝeer and þritty : Genesis v. 1–5, Hereford's text.

99/11. Adam : this word is repeated in H, H_2, H_3, D, D_2, but not in L, which reads, "Adam and."

99/22–24. And alle the sones . . . þre score and fyue : cp. 87/9–12.

XIV. A Prayer at the Elevation.

9. Kyng of au*n*gels, Ioye of seyntis : laus angelorum, gloria sanctorum.

11. Schyner : splendor.

12. Br[ee]d : panis.

13. Vessel of clennesse : vas deitatis.

17. Weye of swetnesse, Trist of soothnesse : via recta, veritas perfecta.

GLOSSARY

aboue, at myn a, in an exalted position, I, 112
Achiliacos, 98/33, *v. Note*
affeffement, estate, possession, VIII, 38; *cp.* med. L. affevatus, affeudamentum, etc. *Not recorded in N.E.D.*
affreyne, *inf.* question, IV, 798
agayne, against, IV, 503
aghttil, *inf.* to direct one's course or endeavours, II, 123
aȝeinbier, redeemer, 59/13
aknowen, *pp.* confessed of, IV, 123
alþir, of all, 84/25
among, *adv.* at the same time, IV, 124; **euer among**, continually, IV, 176
and, if, VIII, 89
a-plight, assuredly, III, 47
askis, ashes, IV, 617
aspie, *inf.* search out, IV, 942; lie in wait (*Vulgate* insidiaberis), 79/36
astert, *inf.* escape, IV, 264; *pt. 3s.* IV, 496
a-stonyd, *pp.* astonished, IV, 81
at, to, III, 24; in, I, 130
a-tamyd, *pp.* tamed, IV, 83
[a]teynt, convicted, VIII, 3
autour, altar, II, 259
a-wreked, *pp.* avenged, IV, 14

balys, *pl.* wretchedness, IV, 318
baysk, bitter, II, 133
bemes, trumpets, III, 76
bere, barley, III, 90
bernacle, bit, IV, 177; *dim. of* O.F. bernac
bete, *inf.* amend, III, 2
bettir, bitter, I, 71
betydde, *v.* bytydde
[biclippyn], *pr. pl.* surround, IV, 156
bidene, together, VIII, 19

bihiȝt, *pp.* promised, VII, 19; bihote, 81/30
biryel, grave, 62/22; **biriel**, 63/30
bismos, fine linen, 96/31, *v. Note*
bitauȝt, *pp.* handed over to, IV, 900
blee, hue, IV, 198
blende, *inf.* confuse, IV, 919; *v. Note*
bloode, bloodshed, IV, 497
blynde, deceptive, VIII, 82
blynne, *inf.* cease, IV, 134
bolde, noble, III, 62; *cp.* O.N. mann-baldr.
bonchef, good fortune, IV, 486
bonde, vassal, IV, 895
boot, *pt. 3s.* bit, 93/33
borion-and, *v.* buriowne
borowe, *pr. 2s. subj.* ransom, IV, 911; *pp.* borowed, II, 55
bote, remedy, deliverance, I, 110; II, 1; **bute**, II, 153; **it is no bote**, it is of no avail, II, 15
bo[un], ready (to go on my journey), VII, 39
bourn, *pp.* born, III, 62
boxom, humble, IV, 247; **buxum**, courteous, noble, III, 30
boxomly, obediently, IV, 360
brade, broad; **vp-on b.**, around, II, 73
bre[c]helnes, frailty, IV, 396; O.E. brycel
brennen, *pr. pl.* burn, 89/25; *pp.* brent, 90/32
brery, thorny, IV, 239
bresid, *pp.* bruised, IV, 18
brest, *inf.* burst, II, 106
briddis, birds, IV, 604
buriowne, *inf.* sprout, put forth, 80/7; *pr. p.* borion-and, III, 90
[burnes], men, III, 34

119

busked, *pt. pl.* prepared, III, 33

but, unless, IV, 31

bute, buxum, *v.* bote, boxom

bynome, *pp.* deprived of, 83/26

byrde, lady, III, 2

byse, fur, I, 116

bytidde, *pp.* **ful woo b.,** wofully afflicted, IV, 96; **betydde,** IV, 272. *The phrase is generally used in impersonal construction*

calamynte, an aromatic herb of the genus *Calamintha,* 95/17

calueren, calves, IV, 539

can, *pt.* did, I, 10; IV, 592; *pl.* IV, 586

canel, cinnamon, 95/17

cawte in clothes, *pt.* 3*s.* swaddled, III, 49

ceesside, cese, *v.* sees, sey[s]en

chace, *imp. s.* drive, IV, 557

chalenge, *pr.* 2*s. subj.* accuse, 60/6

chare, chariot, 89/1

chastied, *pp.* chastised, IV, 68

chaunce, lot, fortune, IV, 631

chese, *inf.* choose, accept, IV, 631

chyuer, *inf.* shiver, I, 35

cleef, *pt.* 3*s.* broke, IV, 405

[c]lere, *pr. pl.* explain, make clear, III, 128

clowte, cloth, shroud, IV, 351

conable, suitable, IV, 138

cordyng, *pr. p.* agreeing, IV, 533

couth, *part. adj.* familiar, at home, IV, 92

couenaunt-briche, breaking of covenant, VIII, 76

creke, a hurdle or bier on which bodies were carried to the grave, IV, 21; *cp.* " cratch," N.E.D. *and* E.D.D.

crocum, saffron, 95/17; *acc. sg. of* L. crocus

crope, *pp.* crept, IV, 912

cruddidist, *pt.* 2*s.* didst curdle, 60/25

cure, do þi c., give thine attention, IV, 773

dare, *inf.* lie hidden in fear, IV, 939

deed, death, 83/14; *gen. s.* **dedes,** I, 88

deede, act, 78/32

deet, debt, II, 228

defaute, lack, I, 117; *pl.* **defautes,** faults, IV, 461

dere, *inf.* injure, I, 74

derworth, dear, IV, 88

dewe, *n.* right, VII, 43

diȝt, *pp.* appointed, IV, 733; dealt with, IV, 637

dikide, *pp.* built, IV, 661

discry, *inf.* describe, III, 129

dis[c]ryen, *inf.* denounce, 99/6

disp[arpl]ye, *inf.* scatter, IV, 938

dissesen, *pr. pl.* molest, IV, 945

doluen, *pp.* dug, buried, IV, 22

dongeoun, castle keep, IV, 661

doo why, *inf.* act so (that), IV, 423; *dat. inf.* **I haue not to doone,** it is not my affair, 84/15; *pp.* **doo,** done, IV, 59

drede, wonder, I, 137, II, 42

dredeful, full of dread, IV, 364

driede, *pp.* drained of blood, IV, 574

dryngles, without drink, II, 284

dyscryue, *inf.* describe, I, 60

echoone, each one, 64/20; **echoon,** VI, 7

eeldid, *pt.* 1*s.* grew old, IV, 58; *pl.* **eldyd,** IV, 106

eft, again, IV, 920

eghe, eye, IV, 57

eisel, vinegar, IV, 590; **eysell,** I, 71

eke, *pr.* 1*s.* add, IV, 261

elke a, each, VII, 13

ellis, if, 87/23

elynges, tedious, lonely, IV, 374; ælenge + -es. *This form is not given in N.E.D., and should possibly be emended to elynge, as in the other texts. Ad. reads* alone, Ro elong

enqwerid, *pp.* examined, 91/22

entencyoun, intention, VI, 64

entent, mind, will, VI, 22

entrikide, *pp.* ensnared, IV, 663

ere, *pr. pl.* are, IV, 225

euen, straight, II, 110

euene, in exact agreement, IV, 704

euerichoon, everyone, IV, 727

eysell, *v.* eisel

faast, firm, strong, II, 18

fare, state, III, 35

faunt, infant, IV, 851
fayn, glad, II, 293
fayry, enchantment, illusion, *translating* Vulgate *illusionibus*, scornings, IV, 249
feer, *inf.* terrify, II, 31; *pr. 3s.*
feri[þ], IV, 736
fele, many, IV, 145, 393
felth, filth, IV, 382
ferde, *pt. pl.* dealt, IV, 309
fere, company, IV, 544; in fere, together, VIII, 99
f[ey], faith, IV, 460
filde, *pp.* defiled, II, 97
fillid, *pt. 3s.* supplied, filled in, 78/27
fleeme, *subj. pr. 2s.* banish, VI, 17; *pp.* flemyd, IV, 838
fli3, *pr. pl.* flee, IV, 685
flum, river, 95/3; flume, III, 102
flyten, *pt. pl.* wrangled, IV, 693
f[o]des, children, III, 53
fonde, *pt. 1s.* found, IV, 141
fonne, fool, II, 63
foorme, *adj.* first; f. fadres, first parents, IV, 259
for, because, IV, 693
force, yeuith no f., attaches no importance, IV, 102
for-do, *imp. s.* do away with, IV, 394; *pp.* [fordon], IV, 8
foreyne, *inf.* wander abroad, VIII, 56; *cp.* med. Latin foraneus, canonicus qui non facit residentiam
forfryede, *pp.* over fried, IV, 572
forslowthid, *pp.* neglected through sloth, IV, 525
forsoke, *pp.* entirely drained of moisture, IV, 571; O.E. for- + sūcan
[forthought], *pt. impers.* it repented me, IV, 292
[for]warde, covenant, IV, 259
for-whi, because, II, 41
for[y]emed, *pp.* despised, IV, 422
fowen, fawn, IV, 830; O.F. foun
fraynd, *pt. pl.* asked, III, 39
frel[e], frail, VI, 7
frely, frailly, IV, 565
frestyng, *verbal n.* proving, III, 73
frith, wood, IV, 830
fulfillid, *pp.* filled full, 63/11
fulsomnesse, abundance, IV, 476

fyn, fee; þou makist þi f., makest terms of peace, VIII, 102

[gamen], mirth, III, 33
gan, *pt. 3s.* did, III, 69
gate, path, II, ł10
glathed, *pp.* made glad, II, 171; O.N. glaða
glo[þer]ed, *pt. pl.* flattered, II, 70
gode, wealth, IV, 339
godesluf-barne, illegitimate child of God, II, 314
goost, spirit, IV, 466
grede, *inf.* cry, IV, 935; *pr. 1s.* IV, 389
grett, *pt. 3s.* greeted, III, 48
gretyn, *inf.* weep, IV, 343; *pr. 1s.* grete, II, 65
grith, peace, IV, 832
gruchchers, murmurers, 99/9

3af, 3ouun, 3yuen, *v.* yeve
3are, readily, III, 33
3ede, 3eden, *v.* yede
3erd, garden, 95/36
3erde, rod, IV, 68, 311
3erne, willingly, IV. 889
3ing, young, IV, 591

[halfundele], half, IV, 737
halle, assembly, hall-moot, or court of the lord of the manor, IV, 71
happily, perchance, haply, 82/4, 92/8
hard, *pp.* heard, II, 125
hardely, assuredly, II, 117
hatte, *pr. 2s. pass.* art called, II, 138; *pt. 3s.* hi3te, 86/31
hawes, oats, III, 89
haylsed, *pp.* greeted, II, 170
heestis, commandments, 85/17
heete, heat, VIII, 123
hele, health, IV, 217, 481; heel, II, 90
hele, *inf.* cover, IV, 151, 395
h[e]nde, hands, III, 77
here-agayne, against this, II, 33
heryid, *pt. 3s.* harrowed, plundered, II, 186
hi3te, *v.* hatte
hirked, *pp.* grown weary, II, 82
holy, wholly, III, 58, 133
homagere, vassal, VIII, 101
hoo, *interj.* halt !, IV, 511

hool, whole, VIII, 111

[h]orowe, filth, pollution, IV, 907; O.E. horu, horw-; *also* horh, phlegm

housel, the Holy Eucharist, XII, 46

hurlyd, *pp.* scarified, torn, IV, 605; (?) *cp.* Sc. harl, to scrape roads with a "harl" or scraper (N.E.D.)

hyle, *imp. s.* conceal, 92/22

into, in (*translating Latin* in *with accusative*), 88/23; **in-to,** to, 88/27; until, 96/26

kerue, *inf.* cut, injure, IV, 728

knowleche, acknowledgment, confession, VI, 66; VII, 34

kydde, well known, IV, 92; manifest, IV, 270

kynde, generation, IV, 642; offspring, IV, 707; nature, VIII, 30

ladde, *pp.* led, IV, 199

lappid, *pp.* wrapped, 63/17

lat, late, *v.* letyn

law, custom, III, 36

leche, physician, IV, 493; **lech,** IV, 131

lende, *inf.* remain, III, 13

lere, cheek, I, 40

lere, *inf.* learn, IV, 283; **[l]ere,** III, 130

lese, *inf.* destroy, IV, 945; *imp. s.* IV, 24; *pt. 3s.* **lees,** lost, 85/8; *pp.* **loore,** VII, 51; **loren,** 64/16; **lorne,** III, 56

lese, *inf.* loose, VIII, 106

lett, hindrance, III, 50; **leet,** III, 51

lett, *inf.* hinder, II, 10

letyn, *inf.* leave, IV, 339; *pr. 2s.* **leetist,** considerest, 61/23; *imp. sg.* **lat,** let, IV, 546; **late,** VII, 15; liberate, 63/31; *pt. 3s.* **lete,** left, IV, 621

leuacioun, elevation, 100/3

leue, beloved, I, 139

leuyd, *pp.* lived, IV, 526

liggiþ, *pr. pl.* lie, IV, 812

liʒtist, *pt. 2s.* didst descend, VII, 46

lisse, *inf.* relieve, IV, 670; **lysse,** IV, 485

lith, joint, IV, 828

loghe, *pt. 1s.* laughed, II, 65

loore, loren, loʒne, *v.* **lese**

lope, *pp.* leaped, fallen, IV, 908

loutid, *pt. 3s.* bowed, III, 50

loue, *inf.* praise, *dant laudem,* 89/34

louely, loving, IV, 131, 493

lowide, *pp.* brought low, IV, 858

lufly, lovingly, III, 130

lust, *pr. impers.* it is pleasing, IV, 669

lykide, *pt. pl.* pleased, IV, 657; *pp.* **lyked,** II, 81

lyme, limb, IV, 828

lysse, *v.* **lisse**

lyueraunce, deliverance, II, 287

malysoun, curse, 81/13

manyon, many a one, IV, 185

mare, more, II, 148

markyd, *pp.* made, III, 20

mathe, worm, IV, 301

meel, time, IV, 739. *The simple noun in this sense does not seem to be otherwise recorded in M.E.*

me[ns]keful, noble, III, 44

mesil, leprous, II, 306

mister, need, IV, 20

mode, mind, II, 298

moght, moth, IV, 301; O.E. mohðe

mooste, *pr. 1s.* must, IV, 107

morne, *inf.* mourn, IV, 124

mote, *pr. 1s. subj.* may, IV, 391; *pl.* **mut,** XII, 28

mouthe, *inf.* voice, IV, 143

mute, assembly, II, 154

mylde, mildness, VIII, 113; O.N. mildi

mynde, memory, IV, 642

mys, fault, VII, 23

mys, *pr. pl.* fail, III, 27

mys, amiss, IV, 172

[mys]fare, misfortune, II, 312

nardum, nard, 95/16; *acc. sg. of* L. nardus

naþeles, nevertheless, 81/19

neghe, *inf.* approach, IV, 146; *pr. pl.* **neghes,** IV, 178

neuen, *inf.* name, III, 11; *pr. 1s.* **[n]eue[n],** II, 4; *pt. 3s.* **neuend,** III, 67

no-kyn, no kind of, II, 304

noon, not, VIII, 92; **non,** III, 27; *not recorded in N.E.D. before* 1651

noot, *pr.* 1*s.* know not, 81/6, 92/21
noyed, *pp.* injured, IV, 643

of, above, VI, 37
omange, among, II, 272
onely, alone, II, 179
oonyd, *pp.* made at one, IV, 704
oord, point, IV, 811
oost, host, IV, 480
or, ere, III, 52; IV, 47, 815; 63/32
[o]**rrour,** hideousness, 64/2; *Vulgate* horror
os, as, I, 151
osprynge, offspring, 93/8
ouȝt, at all, 83/26
outrage, wrong, injury, violence, IV, 477
outray, deed of violence, IV, 110
owe, *pr.* 1*s.* ought, IV, 56

palle, fine cloth, III, 87
passid, *pp.* transgressed, 97/15
pelle[s], furs, III, 87
pelour, fur, I, 116
pertely, straightway, III, 47
peryd, *pt.* 3*s.* appeared, III, 104
pese, *inf.* satisfy, content, VIII, 64
peynt, *pr.* 2*s. subj.* colour, depict falsely, VIII, 7
pight, *pp.* set, IV, 209; **pyght,** IV, 439
plenteuous, plenteous, IV, 826
plete, *inf.* plead, IV, 853
pouert, poverty, I, 114
pouste, power, VIII, 16
poyntes, distinguishing qualities, III, 114
[**poyntil**], pencil, III, 81
prow[t]e, proud, IV, 347; l. O.E. prūt
pure, poor, lowly, II, 8
pyght, *v.* pight
pykide, *pt.* 3*s.* picked, chose, IV, 659
pyne, suffering, punishment, IV, 118

quarte, sound, VIII, 111
quyte, white, IV, 442
quyten, *pr. pl.* requite, IV, 361
qweme, *inf.* please, VI, 15; *pp.* **qwemed,** IV, 418
qwyte, free, IV, 444, 765

ransake, *pr.* 2*s. subj.* search out, 60/11
rathe, early, IV, 299
rede, *n.* counsel, **toke to rede,** decided, III, 37
rede, *imp. s.* counsel, X, 3
refute, refuge, IV, 153
regyoun, realm, IV, 845
remewe, *inf.* depart, VIII, 83
repoort, *inf.* relate, VIII, 79
resen, *inf.* rush, IV, 947
resoort, *inf.* return, VIII, 77
respyte (delay providing) leisure, IV, 446
re[tt]ith, *pr.* 3*s.* imputes, IV, 97
rewarde, *pr.* 2*s. subj.* regard, IV, 793
rewly, wretched, IV, 160
ribauǔ.ie, coarse language, scurrility, VIII, 79
rightwisly, justly, deservedly, II, 45
riȝt, justice, IV, 844
riȝt half, right hand, 62/10
rikenynge, rendering of account, VII, 9
roser, rosebush, III, 43
ruwe, *inf.* have mercy on, IV, 649
ryches, *s.* wealth, I, 114
ryken, *inf.* make payment, VII, 7
ryse (*r. w.* pees), rows, order, III, 116; O.E. ræw. *Cp. York Plays,* XX, 50; Rede youre resouns right on rawes
ryse, brushwood, III, 89

sadde, strongly, IV, 885
saghtil, *inf.* become reconciled, II, 124; reconcile, II, 226
s[aghtyng], reconciliation, III, 75
sale, hall, VIII, 816
sauerist, *pr.* 2*s.* art redolent of IV, 807
sawe, saying, II, 158
say, *pt.* 1*s.* saw, IV, 588; 86/34; *pl.* **sayen,** 97/5; *pp.* **seyen,** 91/2; **sowen,** IV, 674
scheende, *inf.* harm, IV, 644; *pr.* 3*s. subj.* **schende,** IV, 167; *pp.* **schent,** VI, 10; VIII, 45
schene, pure, IV, 467
schewed, *pt.* 3*s.* appeared, III, 63
schopyn, *pt. pl.* shaped, 60/21
schynynge, brightness, 79/18

seche, *inf.* seek, 81/17
see, seat, throne, I, 128; IV, 327
seel, a promise given under seal, IV, 741
seeme, *pr. pl.* befit, VI, 19
sees, *pr. pl.* cease, IV, 511; *pt. s.* ceesside, caused to cease, VIII, 22
seke, sick, II, 251
sekir, *v.* syker
semelaunt, appearance, 89/3
sendel, fine linen, 96/30
sene, visible, I, 8; II, 2; IV, 471
sere, various, II, 9
sete, fitting, III, 10
sett, *pt.* 3*s.* directed, ordered, III, 46
seyen, *v.* say
sey[s]en, *inf.* to put in possession, establish, IV, 951; cese, VIII, 66
silue, same, 61/23
skille, reason, II, 80
skilwys, rational, II, 59
sleeþ, *pr.* 3*s.* slays, IV, 594; *pt.* 3*s.* slou3, 87/13
softid, *pp.* made soft, 60/25
soget, subject, 76/18
soke, *n.* suck, IV, 324
sonnes morne, Sunday morning, II, 187
sotilte, subtlety, IV, 854
sowen, *v.* say
sp[a]ryd, *pt.* 1*s.* refrained, IV, 307
spatil, spittle, I, 70; spotil, 59/6
spedith, *pr.* 3*s.* profits, IV, 133; *pt.* 1*s.* spedde, brought to an end, VIII, 35
sperde, *pt.* 1*s.* shut in, IV, 307; *pp.* shut, IV, 72; *cp.* M.L.G. speren
sperne, *inf.* reject, IV, 895; O.N. sperna
spille, *inf.* slay, 85/7
spiride, *pt.* 3*s.* breathed, 76/29
spotil, *v.* spatil
spryng, *inf.* sprinkle, IV, 441
stall, stable, IV, 430
stede, place, II, 16ι; stide, 80/35; styde, 85/23; steede, II, 206
stede, *pp.* beset, III, 32
stegh, *inf.* rise, II, 200; *pt.* 3*s.* sti3, IV, 687
stere, *pr.* 1*s.* move, stir, IV, 331
steuen, voice, II, 212
stide, *v.* stede
stoode, *pt.* 2*s.* stoodest, IV, 503

stounde, hour, I, 81; hard time, pang, IV, 712
strenghed, *pp.* strengthened, III, 354; O.E. strengan
strenght, *imp. s.* strengthen, IV, 551; O.E. strengðu, *n*
styde, *v.* stede
stynten, *pt. pl.* stopped, I, 47
suffrid, *pp.* borne, endured, IV 802, 809
swelt, *inf.* die, II, 122
swere, *pt. pl.* swore, IV, 612
sweuene, sleep, IV, 702; N.E.D. records no example of this meaning between 1000 and 1645
swilk, such, I, 110
syker, secure, II, 13; sekir, sure, IV, 95
syth, time, II, 48; *pl.* sythis, 99/3

[tarie], *inf.* weary, harass, IV, 608
teermys, limits, 61/28
telth, tillage, cultivation, worship, IV, 384, 500; O.E. tilþ
tene, suffering, IV, 469; XII, 6
[t]erue, *inf.* turn, IV, 726
thank, *n.* to þe most thank, most gratefully, II, 266
ther, *pr. impers.* there is need, II, 123
ther-agayne, against that, II, 18
there, whereas, IV, 166
tho, those, 98/16, 23
thole, *imp. s.* suffer, II, 204; thool, II, 168
throwe, instant, III, 80
tilye, *inf.* till, 86/26
to, till, I, 52; IV, 615, 704; in the presence of, III, 10
to-toorne, *pp.* torn to pieces, IV, 271
to-tuggid, *pp.* torn to pieces, IV, 613
tour, tower, VII, 45
trayn, deceit, IV, 300; *pl.* traynes, IV, 253
trist, *pr. pl.* trust, IV, 125; *pp.* trest, IV, 321
twynnyd, *pp.* separated, VII, 25
tyne, *inf.* lose, II, 143
tyne, *inf.* shut, VIII, 107

þare, these, II, 146
þat, she whom, II, 4
þilk, the same, 84/12
þoo, then, I, 23

þoru-souȝt, *pp.* penetrated, VI, 21;
[þoruȝ souȝt], thoroughly examined, IV, 5; **throgh soght**, IV, 11
þrie, three times, VIII, 85
þriste, thirst, IV, 576

vmbethyng, *imp. s.* bethink, II,
203
vmset, *pp.* surrounded, II, 9
vmthenk, *imp. s.* bethink, II, 177
vndirfonge, *imp. s.* receive, IV, 64
vndirstonde, *inf.* receive, 86/17
vnreste, strife, 79/34
vn-tille, unto, II, 102
vp, upon, IV, 560; [**vp**], IV, 330;
O.E. uppan
vptake, *imp. s.* rebuke, IV, 9, 202;
pp. **vptane**, taken into possession, made my own, II, 89

vagaunt, wandering, 87/36
vertu, divine power, II, 137;
strength, IV, 274
vertued, *pp.* endowed with virtue,
IV, 863. *The earliest example
of this in* N.E.D. *is* 1609
volatils, birds, 76/11

waght, instability, II, 277; *cp.*
O.E. wagian, to totter
walle, well, VI, 32
wanhope, despair, II, 168
wannesse, lividness, *Vulgate* livorem,
88/27
ward, watch, IV, 817
ware, prudent, III, 85
warne, *inf.* refuse, II, 313
warre, worse, II, 50
wasshe, *pr. 3s.* washes, IV, 502;
pp. **wayschen**, VI, 32
wayte, *imp. s.* watch, observe, VIII,
57
wede, apparel, **in w.** *used as expletive*,
III, 16
weer, doubt, IV, 744; **were**, III, 101
w[eie]de, *pt. 1s.* weighed, II, 61
welatesom, disgusting, II, 96
weldant, *pr. p.* ruling, II, 202
weldyng, *verb. n.* wielding, IV, 256

wele, weal, prosperity, VIII, 92
wend, *pt. 1s.* thought, II, 33
were, *inf.* defend, II, 246; *pr. 2s.
subj.* XII, 24
wexe, *pr. 1s.* grow, IV, 212; *pt. 1s.*
IV, 241
whatkyn, what kind of, II, 302
wisse, *v.* wys.
with, by, II, 170, 171
with-**stonde**, *inf.* stand firm, 59/12
wittes, minds, IV, 668
witty, wise, III, 15
w[l]ete, *inf. impers.* cause nausea,
scorn, II, 264; O.E. -wlætan
root of O.E. āwlætan, gewlætan,
to defile; *cp.* O.E. wlātian, to
despise
woltow, wilt thou, VIII, 50
wond, *inf.* turn, IV, 860
wonde, wand, IV, 212
wone, dwelling-place, III, 15
woneth, *pr. 3s.* dwells, IV, 326;
pt. pl. **woneden**, 80/35; *pp.*
wonyd, accustomed, 98/31
wonyng, dwelling, III, 86
woode, furious, I, 141
woodnesse, fierceness, 94/7
woorde, world, IV, 373
worth, *pr. pl. subj.* may (they) be,
IV, 82
wouȝ, wall, IV, 750
wreche, vengeance, IV, 491, 717
w[re]th[l]i, wrathful, IV, 218
write, *pt. 1s. subj.* I, 59
wrye, *pr. pl.* accuse, II, 70. O.E.
wrēgan; *v. Note*
wyk, wicked, II, 68
wyn, joy, III, 54
wys, *inf.* guide, IV, 504; *pr. pl.*
wisse, IV, 668; *imp. s.* **wysse**, IV,
380; **wys**, IV, 399
wyte, *pr. 2s. subj.* blame, II, 269

yede, *pt. 1s.* went, IV, 242; *3s.*
ȝede, 82/5; *pl.* ȝeden, 93/31
[**yeve**], *inf.* give, IV, 295; *pr. 3s.*
yeuith, IV, 102; *pl.* ȝyuen, IV,
171; *pt. 3s.* ȝaf, IV, 324; *pp.*
ȝouun, 76/21

The manufacturer's authorised representative in the EU for product
safety is Oxford University Press España S.A. of El Parque Empresarial
San Fernando de Henares, Avenida de Castilla, 2 - 28830 Madrid
(www.oup.es/en or product.safety@oup.com). OUP España S.A. also acts
as importer into Spain of products made by the manufacturer.
Printed and bound by CPI Group (UK) Ltd, Croydon, CR0 4YY
11/05/2026
02107417-0001